A Place in the Shower Schedule

101 Favorite Columns

By Roger H. Aylworth

DELPHI BOOKS

Lee's Summit, MO

ISBN 13: 978-0-9765185-8-7
ISBN 10: 0-9765185-8-9

A PLACE IN THE SHOWER SCHEDULE: 101 FAVORITE COLUMNS
Copyright 2008 © Roger H. Aylworth

www.DelphiBooks.us

Set in Adobe Caslon By Steve Brooker at Just Your Type

Library of Congress Cataloging-in-Publication Data

Aylworth, Roger H., 1950-
  A place in the shower schedule : 101 favorite columns / by Roger H. Aylworth.
  -- 1st ed.
      p. cm.
  ISBN 978-0-9765185-8-7 (trade pbk. : alk. paper)
  I. Title.
  PN4874.A95A25 2008
  814'.6--dc22
                        2008019621

A Place in the Shower Schedule

101 Favorite Columns

Foreword

I was the editor of a small daily newspaper in the north end of the California's Central Valley when one day I stumbled upon the obvious. Our little paper was doing a bang-up job informing our readers about the events—mostly grim—that took place every day. The problem was that fulfilled only half of our mission.

Back in the Dark Ages, when I got my journalism degree, I was taught a newspaper was to inform and to entertain. Informing we did well, but entertaining was an entirely different matter. Joy, humor, the pleasures of family life, the chance to giggle was just absent from our pages, and I took it upon myself to try to remedy that great failing. Once a week, I would find a way to make people laugh, but it had to be humor people wouldn't be embarrassed to laugh at.

I didn't want biting humor. I didn't want it to be topical. I didn't want to poke fun at politicians, even though they are wonderfully easy targets. What I wanted to do is produce "feel good" humor, situations where people would laugh with and not at other people.

When I looked around for stories that would make people laugh, while not putting anybody down in the process, I had to look no further than my dinner table. My dear bride, the saintly Susan, and I are the button-bustingly proud parents of seven active, intelligent, and sometimes truly nut-ball children. With six sons and a daughter, who is the youngest of the widgets, I realized I had an enormous reservoir of material.

So just as if I had good sense, I dove head-first into the process of producing a weekly column. Each Sunday I gathered a few thousand of my closest friends around my dinner table and I told them stories about the Aylworth clan. They got to know the widgets, and as they grew we added widgets-in-law and later grandwidgets to the character list. As the years passed, the stories changed and the other characters joined the cast, but the essential elements remained the same. During that period, I returned to my first love, reporting, and left the important decisions to others, but I kept the column.

Each week the column made people laugh. They laughed, not because the things that happened in my family were unique, but because they found their families in my words. They all understood what it was to have a teenage son driving the family car, or the madness that could grip a dad watching his baby daughter go on a first date. They laughed because they could see their own kids gather around the toilet for the reverent burial at sea of a goldfish.

Over the years people regularly asked, "When are you going to write a book?"

If pressed, I would explain I was just an aging newspaper reporter while Susan, with seven (soon to be eight) published novels to her credit, is the real writer in the family. However, over the years the question was repeated on a remarkably regular basis. Then one day I looked down and realized I *had* written a book. With something on the order of 780 columns done, I had a giggling history of the clan going back for years.

This is that book. It is a semi-episodic chronicle of a family. Here and there something not entirely related to my blood kin sneaks in like the day I saw the possum resurrected but for the most part, it is us. The volume exists as a celebration of family, as an ode to stories shared around the dinner table, as a testament to what it is to find a place in the shower schedule, when there are nine people living in a house with one bathroom.

I hope you enjoy sharing it with us.

A Place in the Shower Schedule:
Life in a Large Family

A Place in the Shower Schedule

If you think getting tickets to the Super Bowl is tough, try to get a shower in my house.

It's not that showers in the household Aylworth are spectator sports, certainly not with my grand physique.

The issue is one of supply and demand. Simple mathematics: one shower divided by five Aylworths. Combine those numbers with the reality of the bathroom rush hour and you begin to get the picture.

If you want a shower at 3 in the afternoon, you'll probably have no problem but shoot for it during the prime time—I've got . . . to go to school . . . to get to work . . . to get out of this place, and you find that showers are as precious as diamonds.

Another reality is that once established, the shower schedule is more sacred than holy writ. Paul has 5:45 to 6. John takes over at 6. Rebecca has 6:15 to 6:30, and my wife the saintly Susan has staked out from 6:30 on. Any attempt to break in is likely to be met by armed rebellion.

Since my schedule is more flexible—and I'm outnumbered four to one—I end up fitting in as best I can, which means before dawn or after the hot water is gone.

The pre-dawn time slot has the advantage of allowing me to shower in water above freezing cold, but it has its down side, too. For one thing sleep becomes a faint memory. I shoot for a nap, or I go to bed at a time last enforced on me when I was in the third grade. I do hate going to bed before it gets dark.

When I rise up before daylight, good manners demand I try to avoid awakening the saintly Susan. That means selecting the day's wardrobe in the dark. Striped shirts are adorned with flowered ties. Orange and purple socks become a pair. Why not? I've got another pair just like them in my dresser. Taking the late shift is acceptable in the summer, but in January showering in unwarmed water loses some of its charm. Blue is not a good skin color for me and alto screams coming from my bathroom make the neighbors talk.

I suppose we could add another bathroom, but after surviving years when there were as many as nine of us vying for a shower slot, it seems sort of wimpy to go that way now. Besides I don't have a clue where we'd put it. We live in a house that was originally designed as a walk-in closet. A shower in the kitchen would be a bit gauche, right?

Well, maybe someday all the rest of the kids will move out. Or maybe I'll win the Publisher's Clearing House millions.

Until then I suppose I could get a new sprinkler head for the garden hose and make do.

● ● ● ●

A long way from the Poughkeepsie baby factory

I stared at my best buddy Bruce in opened-mouthed astonishment. He had just told me the most disgusting tale I had ever encountered in all my eight years, but there he sat refusing to back up one bit on his story.

He had this odd idea that the making of babies had to do with the . . . well . . . touching and stuff, between men and women. That was silly. I knew as an absolute fact that babies were manufactured in a small factory just outside of Poughkeepsie.

When moms and dads want a baby they send an order to the plant and it takes a bunch of time—about nine months—for the new baby to be prepared. When it arrives, the mom magically knows and she tells the dad and they go to the baby store to pick it up.

It is important to remember I was a child of the 1950s, and my world was so mild that Lucy and Desi never even slept in the same bed. It was also a time when sex was not a topic of discussion in the home. If it weren't for kids like my best friend Bruce, I suspect the entire race would have died out in about 1959 for lack of information on procreation.

Over the ensuing years I learned, if Bruce was a little fuzzy on the details, the boy had the fundamental mechanics of the process more or less correct. Information is—as they say—power, and long before I had any children of my own to confuse, I vowed to see my future widgets got clear, honest, and sensitive information about the birds and bees, information that didn't involve either birds or bees.

When my dear bride, the saintly Susan, and I got into the baby making phase of our marriage, we decided to follow the good advice that you answer the questions the little ones ask and not overwhelm the poor wee beasties with more detail than they can handle.

The problem came when the confusion set in before the questions were asked.

Matthew was our number four widget to arrive and since they came in sort of a tight bunch of years, his three older siblings weren't all that old, either. I remember the morning after Matthew made his debut in the world that I invited all his brothers, at the time all he had were brothers, to come see the little guy.

We got to the window in the newborn nursery and I pointed out the florid bundle of screaming energy in the tiny baby bed in the back, explaining, "That is your brother."

Two of the three were more or less pleased with the new arrival, but Adam, who was about 5, thought dad had clearly lost his mind. From Adam's point of view he was looking into the display window of the baby store and he demanded to know, with all the good ones in there, "Why are you picking that one? There's a way better one over here."

It took a while for Adam to get over my "poor" choice of brothers, but he kind of likes Matthew now.

As the clan grew to seven, I tried to see each of the kids got the right information, and while I avoided ever having a formal "the talk," I think they were better informed than I was. However, there is one exception. If I so much as mention that anything might have to do with the making of babies this boy—I won't say which because he would most likely beat me senseless—recoils.

The idea that his parents ever did more than shake hands is just unthinkable and for the moment he is a lot more comfortable with the plant in Poughkeepsie. I hope he gets this straight before he decides to get married. The shock could kill him.

●　●　●　●

A stamp club admission

I could tell from the look of horror on my daughter's face that I had said too much.

"Dad, you're kidding!"

Becca was truly stricken.

It had never crossed her mind that her father, the man she had loved and respected since infancy, could have sunk to such a distressing level. I tried to explain. I had only made the mistake once, and that was in the eighth grade for crying out loud, but in some things, even once is too many, even if you're in junior high.

I have long maintained the three years from seventh to ninth grade are the most miserable years of human life. It is a time when everything changes and nothing does. In elementary school I was a little kid. Nobody expected more of me. I could be childish because I was a child after all. Then all of a sudden I was in junior high school.

We went from kickball during recess to stripping for gym and taking gang showers without any preliminaries. In grade school, at least officially, all girls had cooties. I had no idea what cooties were, but I was convinced they were to be avoided. Then *POOF!* junior high. The school sponsored dances, and the girls that had all been teddy bears with long hair were wearing make-up and heels.

At the same time I was going through a period when just being awkward would have been a substantial step up the food chain. I was short, chubby, socially retarded and utterly without anything one might call a personality.

My dad still cut my hair and at the best of times I looked like a Q-tip with ears. I was so boring that during lunchtime I hung out with the teacher on yard duty. It was that crying need for some sort of belonging that led me to make the choice that would forever leave me branded.

"I was young! I needed acceptance," I rationalized, but my daughter just gave me a hard look. "Yes, Becca, I admit it. In the eighth grade I was a member of the school stamp club." If I had announced I had been a serial killer, I could not have shaken her worse.

"Dad, only the very worst nerds are in the stamp club! The true geeks!"

It's true. I was a nerd before the word was invented. I wore thick glasses, couldn't dance to save my life, and was a social outcast.

"My father was in the stamp club! If this ever got out I could never show my face in public again! Dad, promise me you will never tell another living soul about the shame you have brought on your family."

"Becca, I did get better. Eventually I even married your wonderful mother," I offered as clear proof of improvement.

"Yeah, well . . . but you still dance weird."

She's right. I survived the eighth grade and by the ninth grade I began to show signs I might someday be human. I grew 5 inches, slimmed down, and learned to dance-after a fashion.

While I never became suave or debonair, I did develop a personality of sorts. I learned to smile. I made friends, dated aggressively, and collected a world full of memories I still cherish.

"Okay, Becca. I'll never tell anybody I was in the stamp club," I promised. You're right; I lied. And, for the record, I still have a small stamp collection that I keep hidden in my bedroom, but heaven's sake please don't tell Becca.

● ● ● ●

'You did this to me'

It was a warm day and I can remember the doctor, at least I think he was a doctor, eating a Popsicle, and I remember that my dear bride, the saintly Susan, didn't like it even one little bit.

The probably-a-doctor and somebody I'm sure was a physician were chatting calmly, right over the top of my wife, and Susan was anything but calm. This was only the second time she had done this, and no matter how you work the facts, every birth is unique unto itself.

We were both a little younger then. I was 23 and my pretty wife was 22. We were living in an apartment that was so far down the residential food chain, that it would have made an outdoor, mountain privy look like good alternative housing. To say we were as poor as church mice would have been offensive to the mice.

Freshly graduated from college, we had made the mistake of exiting school in 1973. It was a time when the national economy had just taken a headlong dive into that mountain privy I mentioned a moment ago.

Our total assets included a beat up old car, a spayed mutt-house cat, named Packy, and toddler named Aaron. By definition having a baby is never strictly speaking convenient, but this delivery was about as ill timed as we could arrange, but nonetheless our soon to be second born was on his final approach.

This was long before every set of parents could resort to an ultrasound to determine what flavor of widget the impending momma had onboard. The baby, who was about to make a scheduled landing on Oct. 9, 1973, was going to be a surprise until the instant of arrival.

We had told Aaron he was going to be a big brother and he was excited as a pre-2-year-old could be about the "baby in mommy's tummy."

Susan had finished finals the spring before, and walked through commencement with the little hitchhiker riding just under her belly button.

From the first day I saw Susan to this very day, I've always been awed by her quiet, but glorious beauty, and in a hot delivery room, in the advanced stages of labor she still managed to be beautiful. However, I don't think she was seeing me as particularly appealing right then.

She had reached, and passed, the "YOU DID THIS TO ME!!!!" stage of labor. She was tired, hungry and in enormous pain, and the dumb guys in the surgical scrubs were eating Popsicles and chatting about things that did not include her.

At that moment in her young life, my beauty was pretty well convinced she should—rightfully—be the absolute center of attention in that delivery room, and random chatting was just not acceptable. What's more she wanted a darn Popsicle and nobody even offered her one.

It wasn't an easy delivery and, while I didn't then and never will fully appreciate what she was going through, I knew the center of my own private universe was in desperate agony.

Finally the little head and shoulders popped out and Adam Anthen Aylworth slipped into the world—hairy, screaming and covered with goo. The presiding physician asked if I wanted to cut the umbilical cord, a significant symbolic act, but I was shaking so hard I was afraid I might do an untrained circumcision on the little guy, so I let the doctor do the snipping.

That was 30 years ago this week.

Adam is a husband and a father in his own right, with widgets of his own, Now, if there is screaming and goo-covered children, he is on the paternal side of the equation.

When Susan has the chance to hug her handsome second born now, or cuddle Adam's adorable dynamos, Anthen and Sydnie, I kind of hope she thinks of me and, with a smile in her heart, says "You did this to me."

● ● ● ●

A moment frozen forever in the amber of time

There are things—and moments in time—that I don't particularly enjoy remembering. For me, most of these have to do with personal or family tragedies; the day of the traffic accident, the airplane that fell out of the sky, or the night a granddaughter left us.

But in every generation there seem to be moments frozen forever in the emotional amber of time, events that by their nature become a shared torture.

We all recall the instant, the place, and astounding details of when and how we got the news. I was sitting in Mrs. Hughes' eighth-grade math class in Herbert Hoover Junior High School, on Nov. 22, 1963, when the school's PA system announced the assassination of President John F. Kennedy.

My folks were staunch Republicans. There was no circumstance under heaven when they ever would have voted for Kennedy, but politics had no importance on that Friday. On that day we weren't Republicans and Democrats. We were Americans, and we all wept for our fallen leader.

Five years ago today my darling daughter, Becca, was playing field hockey for her high school. In the middle of the action she was running to block the on-coming ball, when she crumbled to the grass. In what must be called a freak accident, she had snapped her ankle.

As fearsome as the pain of the break was for my baby girl, I knew that the loss of her senior season with the team hurt immeasurably worse.

Susan and I stayed with her, saw her through the surgery that put a plate and screws into her ankle, and left around midnight after being assured by her doctor we could take her home the next morning, Tuesday, Sept. 11, 2001.

I was up just before 6 a.m. that Tuesday. I wanted my little girl home. I wanted to have her under my roof where I could tend to her needs and try to ease both the physical and emotional pain I knew she was suffering.

As a lifelong news junkie, I flipped on the radio when I stepped into the bathroom. The radio is perpetually tuned to an all-news station, but when the device came to life the voices coming out weren't the newscasters I was used to. In short order I realized the broadcaster in New York City was describing how a plane had crashed into one of the World Trade Center Towers.

Then his voiced changed. This network radio professional with years of training and experience was suddenly screaming. He had just watched another plane, a jetliner, slam purposefully into the other tower.

I ran into the living room to turn on one of the television news networks and then I went into my bedroom to tell my bride, the saintly Susan, something horrible was happening in New York.

I watched television until it was time to get Becca. Hospital discharges always take longer than childbirth, so when I got to her room, I watched her tiny TV, experiencing vicariously the horrors.

At the time I had two nieces living in the Big Apple, where precisely I didn't know, and their fate weighed heavily on me. Hours later we learned from their mom, Susan's sister Patricia, that they were safe, if shaken.

After getting Becca home, she slept—buried under a cloud of pain meds—as I sat transfixed in front of the television.

The day before I had suffered the pains of a daddy, knowing my daughter's heart and body had been wounded. That Tuesday I was reminded what real loss was, and I was so deeply grateful to have my damaged daughter alive and "well" on my couch.

I won't forget that day, and because of it the memory of Becca's injury is etched more deeply on my heart than it might otherwise be. That day is an event no sane person wants to remember, but I fear it is a date no American can afford to forget.

● ● ● ●

On Being Roger

Ancient photo, memories of a 1st grade class

I was going through a box of long-forgotten photographs recently, when I came across some class pictures from my days at West Portal Elementary School.

My darling daughter, Rebecca, on seeing the class pictures instantly came to two conclusions.

"Dad, these kids are soooo 1950s," which came as no big shock, because they were after all, and, "Dad, you are soooo old," which also wasn't necessarily something I needed to hear, but it was unavoidably true.

I look at this collection of widgets and smile.

Up in the corner is Ted. He was half of one of the most non-identical sets of twin brothers I ever met. Glasses, goofy, and adorned with the kind of haircut inflicted by a loving but inept father, Ted is probably the CEO of a Fortune 500 company today, but in 1957 keeping his shoes tied was a major achievement.

On the front row was one of my own personal nightmares. I can't be sure about his name, I suspect the memory lapse is part of some deep set emotional denial. I think his name was Ronny, and Ronny was tough, at least as tough as a runty first grader could be.

He had a stiffly waxed, blond crew-cut, wore brown lace-up boots, a white T-shirt, and blue jeans with folded up cuffs that must have been six inches deep.

Everything about him spoke of 6-year-old swagger, and as I remember he scared the stuffing out of me.

Sitting one row in front of me was the first focus of my pre-adolescent affection, Nancy.

Nancy was perfect in every way. She was blonde and blue-eyed and was so very cute with her missing front teeth. As far as I can remember she never so much as said, "Hi," to me, but even without encouragement I was utterly twitterpated.

Sitting cross-legged on the front row, at the opposite end from Ronny, was Javar. I lived in a modest San Francisco tract home, but my neighborhood was right up against Forest Hills, which was definitely rich man's country. It was also a neighborhood where lots of foreign diplomats lived. Javar was the son of the Indian consul general.

He once promised me he would take me tiger hunting. This was back in the days before anybody heard of the concept of endangered species, and the idea of hunting some beast that could swallow a 6-year-old in a single gulp was heady stuff.

Javar never took me hunting, but if I see him again, I'm going to hold him to his promise, though I'll carry a camera instead of a gun.

Standing in the back row of the photo is Margie.

At age 6, Margie was taller than most of the boys, and had near waist-length "strawberry-blonde" braids. Nobody with a reasonable sense of self-preservation ever called Margie a red-head, because strawberry-blonde or not, Margie had a stereotypical red-head's temper, and a right cross that could stop a charging bull.

Margie and I went all the way through high school together, and she grew into one of the most breathtaking beauties I ever met. For a long time we stayed close and I even attended her wedding, but friendships, like old photos, can fade with passing years.

As I look at the aging picture of Mrs. Biggs' first grade class, most of the faces no longer work their way up to faint memories.

Rebecca declared the kids in the photo were "so cute," and they were, but they lived in much more than a different decade. They lived in a different world, where June and Ward Cleaver were largely real, and Beaver was a kid we all knew because he was us.

●　●　●　●

Line of teachers did more than teach

Recently I found myself pondering the impact of public education on my juvenile mind and my long-term future.

I wasn't thrilled, as a 5-year-old, with the prospect of giving up the free life for the world of academic exploration, and I can still remember the sense of triumph I experienced when I hit upon what I thought was the perfect justification for taking a pass on this whole school thing.

I proudly walked in to my mom to explain, "I can't go to school. I don't know how to read!" My parents were not sympathetic, and off to school I went.

In third grade I fell in love with an older woman. I suppose there never was any real hope for my teacher, Miss Lewis, and me. After all she was just about twice my height, but I was smitten and blind to the little obstacles.

My heart was broken just before school ended for the summer, when Miss Lewis announced she was going to get married, would have another name, and was leaving the school. I realized then and there, life isn't fair, and I vowed never again to fall for a woman more than two feet taller than I am.

In the sixth grade terror set in when I realized I was going to be in the class of the notorious **MRS. HAZEL SULLIVAN!** Mrs. Sullivan was endowed with a crisp New England accent and the capacity to wither even the most rambunctious pre-adolescent with a single look.

We learned that, while Mrs. Sullivan apparently hated children in general, she loved and cherished her class. It was a secret we all tacitly agreed to keep among the in group of her students. Let the rest of the school cower as she passed. We knew Mrs. Sullivan was a pussycat.

I remember the parents' night when Mrs. Sullivan confided in my folks, "I don't know what Roger will do for a living, but it will have something to do with writing."

I knew she was wrong because my career path was set. I was going to be a chemistry teacher. It was the era of "Mr. Wizard" on television, and from my point of view, there was simply nothing cooler than working with chemical magic.

That of course was before I met Mr. G. T. Wolf, the chemistry instructor at Abraham Lincoln High School. Rumor had it Mr. Wolf's initials stood for "Gray Timber," which may or may not have been true, but what was absolutely certain was the pretty blonde who sat behind me in class was materially more interesting than anything Mr. Wolf could possibly say.

The result was a "D" in chemistry, which I well and truly earned, and a radical re-thinking of career paths.

This led me to Mrs. Blennerhassett, a wonderful, grandmotherly woman who was in charge of my high school's history department. I loved history and was thrilled when she made me her teaching assistant. I even graded tests for her.

I recall grading one California history exam where one inventive—if unlearned—student identified "Mother Lode" as "a nice old lady, who lived in the foothills."

I knew then I would be a high school history teacher, the weird guy who loved things old and dusty, but who could enthrall my students in the sweep and splendor of the past.

It was the fall of my senior year that I met Mr. Taylor.

Mr. Taylor, who had a first name and hated it, taught my high school's journalism classes. He had always longed for nothing more than to be a newspaper reporter but fate and circumstance intervened. He had become a teacher instead, but his love for the trade never ebbed.

With the passion of a southern preacher, he taught us that journalists were the noble knights-errant of the age. They could change the world, cure the ills of society, and one at least was faster than a speeding bullet and could leap tall buildings at a single bound.

His passion and enthusiasm were contagious, and the scum-sucking-pig-dog infected me. I am yet to find a cure. I'm still not sure whether I love or hate that man, but I will never forget him or what he gave me.

● ● ● ●

Passing from groovy to 'tragically unhip'

Back in the dark ages—way back before cell phones, MTV, and the Internet—I was officially "groovy."

There were times I even attained the status of being "far out!" I knew the names of all the popular bands. I went to rock concerts at Winterland and the Crystal Ballroom, and if you have to ask where they were, you're just too young to care.

I sat a few feet away from Janis Joplin as she sang. I stared in open-mouthed, adolescent adoration at Grace Slick, who I was convinced was the most beautiful woman of the age, an age that has well and truly passed.

I could—and usually did when I was alone—sing along with every song that played on the radio. That's when radio meant the AM band and the only station a San Francisco kid listened to was "THE ROCK OF THE BAY!"

I knew what a "Peter Max smile" was. I knew Ed Sullivan wasn't cool, even if he did host the Beatles on his show.

Despite the commonly repeated lament—usually made by envious members of hopeful garage bands—that they weren't a "real" band, I still liked the Monkees.

I knew the difference in meaning between "far out" and "FAR OUT!!!!"

I was in with the in-crowd. I was uptight and out-of-sight, when being uptight was still a good thing.

I even surfed until a fickle ocean tried to kill me for no good reason I could see.

I skateboarded when skateboards were a recreation, not a lifestyle.

I wore white Levis, wide-striped shirts and low-top, black Converse tennies.

I could do the "Swim," the "Pony," the "Jerk," and, when "oldies" were playing, I could revert to the "Twist."

I knew girls were "chicks," and any woman under the age of my mother wanted to be thought of as a "girl."

I knew what Carnaby Street was, and I was convinced any chick with an English accent was groovy.

But all of that was then, way, way, way back then, and now—well—now I'm not nearly so far out. I had that point driven home recently.

A group of my colleagues and I were headed to a training session 100 miles away and we were carpooling.

When I asked Bill, the paper's head photographer, about space in his truck he said, "OK, but I hope you like Eminem."

"Bill, I don't eat M&Ms. I have to avoid chocolate," I innocently responded.

Everybody in earshot stopped and looked at me as if I had just belched in the middle of a funeral.

"Roger, you are tragically unhip," offered Heather, another colleague, who then explained, in terms reserved for small children or the mentally challenged, that Eminem is a performer.

I thought this was all sort of funny, but I was yet to get the difference in spelling between the candy and the singer, and I also was under the misimpression that Eminem was a band.

So when I wrote my dear bride, the saintly Susan, an e-mail about the encounter, I told her about the band M&M.

"Sorry, Love, but you are still tragically unhip. The solo rapper is Eminem," Susan wrote back.

OK, I guess we have hard proof. I am "tragically unhip," but I can still do the Pony—after a fashion.

● ● ● ●

Tuxedo can add 'Woo! Whoo!' to the world

Officially and for the record I want to state emphatically, I love my tux.

About a decade back a conjunction of two widget weddings and an invitation to a presidential inauguration made it economically appropriate to purchase rather than rent a tuxedo.

Since then, generally found hiding in a back corner of my closet, I have had my own personal tux.

It is your basic "the-name-is-Bond, James-Bond" black tux with cummerbund. There are no wild colors, no iridescent bow ties. It doesn't have any embroidery. In the world of tuxes this bit of apparel is about as mundane as they come.

But I have discovered something: There is nothing mundane about a black tux.

I need to confess what is obvious to anybody who knows me. I'm not what most women would call pretty.

It's not that I have to sneak up on mirrors or small children run screaming when they see me coming down the street, but I'm not Brad Pitt, or Mel Gibson, or, more to the point in this case, I'm not Sean Connery. However, the wonder of the tux is you don't have to be pretty.

I recently had good cause—at least I thought it was good cause—to pull my tux out of the closet and wear it to work.

At the best of times a newspaper office is not the epicenter of sartorial splendor, so that might play a role, but every woman in my office had something nice to say about the outfit.

One of my colleagues—I won't say who so she doesn't have to explain this to her hubby—actually came to her feet and shouted, "Woo! Whoo! Don't you look good!"

I don't get a lot of "woo! whoos!" on an average work day, so this was a fun experience.

It is the case that I am the most happily married man I know, and the fact my dear bride, the saintly Susan, loves me is about all the ego stroking I could ever ask for.

However, I have enough of a male ego to be pleased that members of the softer side of the species—older, younger, single, married, or any combination of the above—took time to look and express appreciation for me and my attire.

The other proof the outfit works was the male response.

While most guys, the secure ones, just sort of smiled, a few responded in . . . well, less admiring ways.

There was the guy who asked if I was the head waiter, and another who said I reminded him of a penguin.

I understand both comments, and they could both be meant as amusing observations, but I think they were blatant examples of tux envy.

You can't wear a tuxedo every day. It loses its impact pretty fast. So my black wool friend is back hiding in the closet, but I'm not going to give up on my buddy.

It's nice to know that elegance and a touch of romance still have their place in the allegedly modern world. And it is nice to know that "woo! whoos!" do, too.

●　●　●　●

Defining love and plausible deniability

Don't tell anybody, but I think there is a reasonable chance one of my widgets is falling in love.

With four single children (three of the seven in the original herd are already married), there is a fairly good chance somebody is falling in love in my household at any given moment. However, in this particular case I think I see the signs of early-stage twitterpation.

For the most part, I am a fan of being in love. I've been hopelessly, head over heels, crazy-mad about my dear bride, the saintly Susan, for more than three decades, and I don't see any likelihood that will change as long as I continue breathing. At the same time falling in love is one of the most bizarre experiences of life.

It never happens in the same way twice.

Even though most of us have been in love, some times more than once, we can no more define the emotion than we can catch sunshine in a feather duster.

When I was young—and while my children will debate the issue, I was young once—I could fall in love with three different young beauties in the time it took me to walk from my math class to English.

Bright eyes, a passing smile, and I was smitten. If she went so far as to say, "Hello," I was ready to climb any mountain, swim any sea, face any danger, as long as the mountain wasn't too high, the sea was warm, and the danger wasn't really scary.

As often as not, when a girl turned out to be smitten with me, an event that occurred with enough regularity to keep me from utter adolescent despair, I would miss it entirely.

I could no more define love then than I can now, but I knew it was something I wanted to be in.

That youthful quest led me to a series of broken hearts and encouraged me to write some of the sappiest entries in my journal that any teen ever dribbled onto paper.

It is that drivel that to this very day has kept me from letting any member of my family read my high school journal. But drivel though the words may have been, the emotions were real, and the heart aches hurt just as bad as if the loves were anything more than high school infatuation.

Oddly, when I found the real thing I could define it no better.

I could never tell you why I adore the saintly Susan other than it was the only right thing to do.

We used to sit on the porch outside of her dorm when the evenings were pleasant, and I was too broke to take her someplace more interesting.

We would talk and giggle and she would rub my back. Then something magical happened.

I won't say which widget seems to be on the teetering verge of finding that same magic.

Getting privacy of any sort around my house has always been difficult and it is a lot tougher if your old fat dad is spreading your fledgling love-life all over the newspaper.

Also in case I'm wrong I want to leave the poor kid a level of plausible deniability. (I don't know what that means either, but it is something a former CIA officer once said to me and I've always wanted to work it into a column.)

I also know if this particular match-up is not the one that will make the magic that lasts forever, that the magic is still real, and if they are blessed, all of my widgets will someday find the magic their parents have enjoyed for all these years.

●　●　●　●

'That's my story and I'm sticking to it!'

Not long ago the people with titles in my office forced me into the annual torture of a "personnel review." Every year, more or less in the general vicinity of my anniversary date, my bosses take time to ask, "What's up with Roger?"

In fairness, that is not a particularly unreasonable question. In point of fact, it is a question I ask myself almost daily. However, when my bosses ask this particular question, it takes on a special significance. After all, my continued employment in the hallowed confines of the newsroom hangs on the hook of this inquiry. Candidly, I'm inclined to believe that I would have to do something extraordinarily stupid to find myself among the unemployed. Having said that, I must confess that extraordinarily stupid is not beyond my capacity to achieve. At any rate the annual evaluation process is a multi-step procedure in this asylum, and the first part is always the hardest.

My immediate supervisor, a genuinely pleasant fellow named Steve, who long ago realized giving me orders is roughly as simple as herding cats, walks over to me and plunks an "employee self-evaluation" form on my desk. The form includes a number of salient questions asking about my work habits, desk neatness, personal hygiene, and whether I work and play well with others.

The hard part is my bosses seriously expect me to sit down and evaluate myself, in writing, and then give this handwritten confession to them so they can beat me with it. To my mind, this concept is right up there with the father who tells his miscreant offspring, "Go and find something I can beat you with!"

My Dad, with very good justification, smacked my behind from time to time in my rug-rat years. He never beat me, but if he had, the man would have had the good sense to choose his own implement. If the choice was left up to me, I'd have run out and grabbed a blade of green grass, or better still a pigeon feather, and on handing it to my Pop, I'd have said something like, "Here, knock yourself out."

So here I have a form where I need to identify all my faults and foibles and to "use additional space, if needed." I know full well, I am not now and I never will be anything in the vicinity of perfect. There are days when I have a hard time working my way up to mediocre, but at the same time there are other days when—in all humility—there aren't six people in the time zone who can do better what I do.

I do want to improve at my chosen profession. As silly as it sometimes sounds, I'm proud of what I do for a living. There are times when reporters have changed the world for the better. I'd like to honestly plead guilty to achieving that now and again. So faced with the evaluation form, I do what every reasonable person would: I admit obvious faults, overstate whatever strengths I can identify, and obfuscate on any question that scares me. If challenged, I'll respond with the ever-lame, "That's my story and I'm stickin' to it!"

Ultimately, I'm convinced self-evaluation is a daily ritual, and while failure is painfully obvious, success can be much more difficult to discern.

● ● ● ●

When I get older, losing my hair, many years from now

It was nostalgic, wonderful and more than a little strange.

As the band's familiar music blasted out over the packed concert hall, "girls" danced in the seats and aisles, people clapped in time to the music and when they reached the famous chorus, the entire hall erupted in a deafening "YEAH! YEAH! YEAH!!!" I sang—or more accurately screamed—right along with the rest of the crowd.

Since I was in my mid-teens—long, long ago in a galaxy far, far away (San Francisco, to be exact)—I have enjoyed rock music and from time to time attended rock concerts.

I've been to concerts featuring everybody from the Cowsills to Janis Joplin, and from the Beach Boys to Herbie Albert and the Tijuana Brass, but on a more recent Saturday night, with my best girl and dear bride, the saintly Susan, by my side, I was sitting a few rows back from the stage waiting to be thrilled.

It wasn't the venue or even the music that made this concert out of the ordinary. It was the audience.

Instead of a roomful of teens, this hall was filled with people who could eat off the seniors' menu, and instead of trendy clothes and belly button rings, this crowd sported orthotic shoes, "relaxed-fit" clothing and hearing aids—turned way down. This was a concert aimed at people who danced the "Twist" when they and it were both new.

The featured act for the night was a band called "Rain," a group of five talented musicians who make their living by "being" The Beatles. They do a remarkable job, complete with appropriate costumes and *ersatz*-Liverpool accents. I suspect none of the performers was even alive when the Beatles first got together, and yes there are five, but one sort of stays in the shadows and runs the synthesizer while the others are the "Fab Four."

There is a secret we try to keep from our children. We want them to think we are mature adults, after all, but inside any gray-haired old duffer there lurks a 16-year-old, waiting to pop out.

For the most part wisdom and a healthy desire for self-preservation keep my inner teen in place. From time to time I have let him sneak out, usually during pickup football games with my widgets, and when I make that mistake I pay for it in good, honest pain.

On this night. the situation allowed the teen not only to sneak out but to romp around. When Paul McCartney—no it wasn't really Paul—urged us to get up and dance, I danced, after a fashion. When they played "She Loves You," they couldn't have kept the crowd from screaming "YEAH! YEAH! YEAH!!!" on cue.

I suspect the band keeps the volume way up, not just for the hard of hearing, but to make sure the sound of the dancers' creaking joints doesn't drown out the music.

But it doesn't matter. This was a moment when boomers could be more nearly babies again.

When a much younger couple—probably in their 20s—sat next to me, I jokingly said there was an age limit, a bottom limit, for this concert and they were clearly way too young.

The guy looked at me as if he thought I was nuts, which I suppose was a reasonable reaction, but the woman said, "It's OK, I dye my gray hair."

Who knew?!

That night was all about memories and being what we remembered we were, but the band missed one song I really expected:

When I get older, losing my hair, many years from now,
Will you still be bringing me a Valentine, birthday greetings, bottle
of wine?
If I've been out 'til a quarter to three, will you lock the door?
Will you still need me, will you still feed me,
When I'm sixty-four?

● ● ● ●

Widget Wars

How do you parent?
Simple question has no easy answer

I had just come staggering out of the gym—it had been a serious rump-buster of a workout—when I saw a young mom herding a trio of little boys, ranging in age from about 6 to 2, across the parking lot. The youngest one burst into the lot out without the benefit of a hand to hold.

"Caleb, hold your brother's hand!" said mom sternly.

Not being shy, I chimed in, "Listen to your mother, Caleb, or you'll end up squished flatter than a piece of paper!"

Caleb immediately grabbed his brother's hand, while his mother turned and looked at me, obviously wondering who this truly strange man was.

"This looks really familiar to me," I said by way of explanation. "I've got six sons of my own."

She stopped and looked at me in unabashed astonishment.

"What are their ages?" she asked.

"Well, I've got a daughter too, and the seven of them range from 35 to 22 1/2."

"Then you can give me some advice. How do you parent?"

She might just as easily have asked me to explain quantum mechanics or provide a brief overview of unified field theory.

Even though I have been a parent for more than half of my life, I can't say I have a clear idea of how to be a parent.

Part of the problem is widgets don't come with an owner's manual. What's more, there is no standard-issue kid. Each one of the little crumbgrinders, from the moment he or she first starts beating on the inside of mommy's tummy, is as individual as snowflakes.

Also, and this sounds weird, no two children—even identical twins—are born into the same household.

When our senior son, Aaron, made his arrival into the brave world, Susan and I were dirt-poor university students, who regularly had to search the couch to find enough pennies to buy stamps for the bills we could pay that month.

Each successive addition to the clan finds a world changed by his or her arrival, if nothing else.

Matthew, kid four in the mob, forced Susan and me to make the leap from apartment dwellers to homeowners because we couldn't begin to figure out how to jam ourselves, and four little boys, into a two-bedroom apartment.

Also each kid teaches his or her parents new things.

Aaron taught us that a box of animal crackers can keep a wee one entertained long enough to finish the grocery shopping.

Paul, number six among the boys, taught us to be very specific in giving instructions. Who knew you had to tell a kid not to jump off the roof of the barn with a black garbage bag as a parachute?

Another inescapable truth is boys and girls are different.

Becca, the last of the seven and our only girl, was unique in a whole bunch of ways beyond plumbing. She's always been as emotionally and intellectually strong as her brothers, and had a right hook that wouldn't quit, but she is also a girl in every sense of the word.

While she had never seen a baby doll until she was given one on her first birthday, she knew to hug and cuddle it the minute it came out of the box.

I know that children have to know you love them, even when they have just backed your Mustang into a steel pole.

I also have learned, as often as not, kids aren't the least bit interested in advice when they come to you to get some. What they want is to know you think their worries, thoughts, ideas and problems are worthy of being listened to.

I've learned that parents have to act like grownups, even when they don't want to.

I know that smalls need parents, not just older friends, and they like to know where the boundaries are, even when they still want to push on them.

I know nothing makes a kid feel more secure than knowing mommy and daddy love each other, even if they express that love loudly sometimes.

I also know I don't know how to parent, but sometimes I have a clue how to be a daddy, a dad, and even a father. Now, I'm learning to be a grandpa.

● ● ● ●

When vacations were trials by ordeal

I'm utterly exhausted, every available bone in my whole entire body aches, and I'm completely brain dead, which is all understandable because I just got back from a vacation.

Vacations are great things. I look forward to them with genuine child-like glee, but I have begun to realize that a person needs to take some time off to recover from so much fun.

When the household widgets were small, Aylworth family vacations took on near-mythic proportions. Even now, when my adult-size children gather around the family dinner table for some sort of an occasion or celebration, the long-ago trips are often a topic of conversation, and those vacations have developed shorthand nicknames.

"Hey remember the taxi crash trip?"

"What about the camping vacation when we spent most of our time in the emergency room?"

"How about the vacation when we all got a ride in the highway patrol car?" Don't ask.

"Remember the time the van kept breaking down?"

To that question there is only one answer, "Which time?"

There was the vacation when Matthew had an emergency appendectomy.

There was the trip when we stayed in the place with two stuffed alligators in the lobby.

There was the time we stuffed the entire family into an alleged motel room that wouldn't have made a good-sized walk-in closet, and ended up paying an arm and a leg for the privilege because Yellowstone National Park was full and this was our only option.

Our vacations all tended to be made on a shoestring budget, and usually driving vehicles that sane people wouldn't have trusted to make it across the street.

Because of financial and time constraints, the trips were limited.

Often the journeys became trials by ordeal, where we tried to cram more miles, more sights, and more "we are going to have fun on this trip or die in the attempt" than anybody not living in a sit-com would even consider.

Also driving times, or at least the time to start a trip, was dictated by the functioning of the car's air conditioner, which was usually non-functional. If we were headed somewhere that was hot, or going through someplace that was hot to reach our destination, then night driving became a necessity.

While the family made numerous trips that required we traverse Nevada in the summer, none of my kids ever saw Nevada until they were in their late teens, because they always made the journey snoozing as we cruised along in the darkness.

Other times we planned our routes not by the quickest or the most scenic option, but based on the way that had the most population in case we broke down.

We learned how to make sandwiches for nine as we rumbled down the road because a Big Mac would have been the budgetary last straw.

Even with the budget considerations, we made a couple of amazing trips.

The whole family recalls both trips we made deep into Mexico.

Once with all seven of our own wee beasties in tow, and a nephew we added to the crew just for jollies, we found ourselves in a tiny fishing village on the jungle coast of western Mexico.

My dear bride, the saintly Susan, and I had temporarily left the brood to the care of the older brothers in the hotel room and strolled in the tropical sunset down to the town square for a few minutes of relative peace.

We were sitting in the raised square when a fellow American came up to us. He said he had seen Susan and me, with the widgets, in a local restaurant earlier in the evening.

"I'm a freelance photographer," he said, and explained he had covered wars, revolutions, and natural disasters all over Central and South America.

"I've got to tell you, you are the bravest people I have ever met," he said.

I had thought the kids were on their best behavior in the restaurant, but I thanked him and he walked off shaking his head.

Since the early days of family vacations, our budgets and our vehicles have improved. In recent years our trips have been marked more with successful travel than tales of disaster.

I still find I need a few days after a vacation to recover from all that much fun and frivolity, and get back into the swing of being a taciturn newspaper reporter, but now it is more a response to over-aggressive recreation than overt battle wounds.

At some level I think I like the more successful trips we make these days, but I have to admit the old trips made for better after-vacation stories.

● ● ● ●

Widgets come with their own weirdness

One of the things being the father of a small army provides me—aside from gray hair—is hard evidence that widgets arrive with their own unique and sometimes fairly odd personalities.

From the sleep positions the wee ones prefer, to whether they would rather eat squished peas or that gag-ya rice cereal that we inflict on our kids, each comes with preferences, likes, dislikes and pure weirdness.

When my son, Adam, who is now a married daddy, was just out of the rug-rat phase, his greatest joy in life was to join his big brother, Aaron, for the vast adventure of walking three blocks to the neighborhood store. While Aaron was intent on collecting all the candy 25 cents would buy, Adam wanted only one thing—a fist-sized kosher dill pickle.

Matthew, son number four in the family group, had a fixation that I still don't begin to comprehend. When he was a curly-headed 18-month-old with a big gap-toothed grin, Matthew had an unexplained compulsion to steal catsup bottles.

The little guy would hang around the kitchen. When his mother, my dear bride the saintly Susan, opened the refrigerator. Matthew would dash up, snatch the catsup bottle out of the door, and run giggling to the back bedroom.

We never had a clue what—or if—he was thinking. He never ate the catsup. He never used it as finger paints, and we never found any evidence he was dousing the dog or the cat, but he really wanted that bottle.

When my son, John, was in his middle teens, he decided he wanted a pet of his very own, and promptly captured a black widow spider, which he named Queen.

Queen lived in a large mayonnaise car on his window sill. Not to be outdone, John's older brother, Jared, caught a black widow of his very own, Stalin, who lived in an adjacent bottle. Things went well until the brothers got to the "my spider can beat your spider" discussion and the two arachnids found themselves in the same bottle. Stalin overthrew the Queen and she became the guest of honor in the bathroom for a formal burial at sea.

Reaching the status of a grandfather has proven to me that widget peculiarities are not limited to my own kids.

Sydnie, the oldest daughter of my son Adam and his dear bride Dana, is a blue-eyed, blonde, 3-year-old cherub, with a smile that can melt lead or a grandpa's heart with equal ease.

Sydnie likes to visit public restrooms. The little darling, who is more or less housebroken, has no interest in using the facilities. She just has a thriving fascination with the fixtures.

She's a special fan of "magic bathrooms," the ones equipped with the sensors that flush toilets and turn on sinks without touching handle or spigot.

Given the choice Sydnie would rather visit restrooms than go to a circus. I found this out when I took her to the circus.

Her older brother, Anthen, 5, is a two-legged dynamo, who could easily power several small countries. He also makes a sound— he says he is whistling but that is open to serious debate—that at close range can stun an elephant into stupor and from a little further away can be used to etch glass.

At the same time, Anthen genuinely hates really loud noises, so he covers his ears when he "whistles."

So do I.

My Daughter, the teen

In a handful of days my lone daughter is going to change into that most frightening of all earth's inhabitants—a teen-ager. The concept of having a teen-age girl under my roof is overwhelming.

Having teens in the house is not that big a shock. All of Becca's six brothers are or were at one time teen-agers. In fact there was one three-day stretch when I had five teen-age sons. But the keyword there is sons.

I have some understanding of teen-age boys—after all, I was one. Despite the fact they are a seething caldron of emotions, laced liberally with raging hormones, they remain essentially predictable. Teen male goals are simple, basic, more a matter of cave-instinct than intellectual exercise. This I understand. My wife, the saintly Susan, reminds me periodically that I haven't progressed much beyond that level myself.

But Becca is not a he. She is a she, a fact I found mildly shocking every time I changed her diaper. Girls simply are different from boys and the difference runs deeper that just plumbing. At the same time the sure knowledge that I have some understanding of the junior members of my own sex is part of what keeps me nervous.

You see, somewhere there is Scott. I have never met Scott. He might be a nice young man, but he has a fatal flaw. He likes my daughter. I certainly understand why a male would find my daughter attractive. Becca is frighteningly intelligent, talented, and utterly beautiful. She is endowed with a gentle heart and a playful disposition, but she is also my little girl and I own a shotgun.

I consider all males suspect, and anyone specifically interested in my darling daughter automatically upgrades from suspect to target. Becca just giggles when I mention Scott, and that makes matters worse.

Scott is one of four boys and three girls she has invited to her 13th birthday party and the paired-off nature of the numbers hasn't entirely escaped my notice.

At the same time I don't really know what Becca is thinking about Scott, or anything else. In point of fact I have no way of predicting teen-age female behavior.

I had no clue what teen-age girls were thinking when I was part of the same time zone. The logic, the entire mental process of a teen-age girl, was a mystery to me. With a gulf of 26 years stretching between my here and now and the last time I was a teen-ager, the chance for understanding seems slim.

Sometimes Becca is a young lady of maturity and grace. She has a long, black-lace dress that she wears to special occasions and she is devastating in it.

Other times she is something of a looney-tune.

A while back she came up with a gouge under her arm.

"How did that happen, Becca?"

"Well, I was wondering what it would be like to be blind. So I was walking down the street with my eyes closed and ran into a street sign."

Okay, that makes sense to me.

She will sneak up behind me and tickle me unmercifully. Should I turn and bark at her, she responds with a big, trembling pouty lower lip and silent tears trickling down her cheeks. No daddy anger can survive the pouty lower lip for long, let alone the tears.

For the next seven years I'm going to have a teen-age girl in the house. There is no good way around it, but I do have one question: Do you think a fat, talkative, newspaper editor could find a spot in a monetary for, oh, about seven years?

● ● ● ●

Sister knows how to survive among six brothers

I know it sounds a bit odd, but I have never been entirely sure if my darling daughter, Rebecca, has been spoiled or abused, and I suspect she isn't too sure either.

Becca arrived 16 1/2 years ago to round out a family group that included six older brothers. Boys in general and brothers in the specific have been part of her everyday life since she took her first breath. That has led to a fairly rough and tumble lifestyle.

Until she was five and went to kindergarten, our one and only female widget thought all girls came with six older brothers as standard issue. In school she discovered some kids had fewer male siblings, almost nobody had more, and others had girl siblings—yes, sisters—and still others were only children, an idea I think she still can't entirely grasp.

Being the youngest and the girliest never apparently daunted my little blue-eyed doll.

She learned early on she'd get almost anything from her brothers—or her dad for that matter—with a smile and a "Becca-hug." When it came to her male siblings, if she couldn't win the day with persuasion, or a Becca-hug, she wasn't above physical intimidation.

I remember one morning when Becca and her senior brother, Aaron, who is 12 years older, were having an argument in the hall. I couldn't tell you what it was about to save my life, but Becca was about four, and not much over three-and-a-half feet tall, and Aaron was a six-foot-plus, 16-year-old. Whatever the cause, Becca pulled back her sturdy little fist and let go with a jab at just her shoulder height, which means on Aaron the punch landed . . . well, you know where the punch landed, and Aaron toppled like a fallen oak.

When I got to the scene of the assault, Aaron was curled up and moaning on the floor, and Becca was standing over him with hands on both hips and a decidedly smug look on her cherubic little face.

At the same time Becca is absolutely a girl. When she was not much more than a toddler, she used to change clothes 14 times a day. Now she is woman high, she sparkles in jeans and T-shirts, and can be utterly elegant in a formal. That doesn't mean her brothers have forgotten she is their "baby" sister, and they can be protective in their own slightly psychopathic way.

Becca is planning to take a young man from Washington to a girl-asks-guy dance at her high school. The brothers, being very alert, recognized they had not had a chance to meet or approve of the Washington lad. So failing the opportunity to approve, they decided to go right to intimidation.

According to the plot, this collection of loving brothers intended to track the couple to their restaurant of choice and then to "explain" to the lad how dearly they adore their baby sister, and how unhealthy it would be for her to have any sort of a negative experience in his company. Abject, reverential terror was the simple goal. A wife of one of these brotherly Neanderthals got wind of the scheme and alerted Becca, who in turn reminded her male siblings what she once did to Aaron and they all thought better of the idea.

I know Becca adores her brothers, and the wives and children of the married ones. I also know the seven of my kids have all taught each other lessons I never could have delivered.

Becca needs very little protection, but her dates might.

● ● ● ●

Control: You can't lose what you never had

There comes that moment in a father's life when he stands looking heavenward and asks, "Where did I lose control?"

That moment came to me last week. OK it wasn't the first time in my parenthood that moment came, but it was the most recent arrival.

After more than two years of separation, my youngest son, Paul, returned to home and hearth. Paul, 21, who has spent the last 25 months in Texas working on some genuinely important projects, finally came home.

During his absence our communication has been limited to letters and a few rare phone calls, so it was really good to have him back inside the Casa Aylworth.

I was reveling in getting to know him again, the big kid with the goofy smile, who has been replaced by an amazingly matured young man, although he still is blessed with the big goofy grin.

Well, I had not much more than settled down with him to say, "Hi, howya doin'?" when I handed this person the keys to our brand new car, pointed him two states east, and said, "Go get your sister."

The sister in question—the only one in the fam, for crying out loud—is my darling daughter, Rebecca.

My Becca is just finishing her freshman year in college and she needed a ride home, so my dear bride, the saintly Susan suggested we send Paul to do the collecting.

At first blush it sounded like a good idea.

Susan and I both have to work. Paul is momentarily between jobs. Becca and Paul, aside from being siblings, are dear friends—heck, it's probably been two and a half years since either last threatened great bodily harm on the other—and somebody had to bring the poor girl home.

I suppose theoretically, we could have just sent the dear daughter a plane ticket and met her at the airport, but when she went to school last fall she took everything but the kitchen sink, and she may have sneaked that out too. To fly Becca and her stuff home would probably require we charter the entire aircraft, and that commences to get expensive right early on.

So all in all, Paul seemed to be the natural choice, but just because something seems rational doesn't mean it makes one tiny little bit of sense.

Despite the calendar, the weather still thought it was winter. The drive is a grueling brain-fryer. It's tough enough to stay conscious on this trip with a companion, and Paul was going solo.

To give him any real chance of getting there at all, we gave Paul the keys to his mother's brand new, much loved little car, which she has named Beethoven, and since he has no money, we stuck a credit card in his hand—our credit card—pointed him east and said, "Bye-bye."

OK, we sent a single, healthy, active 21-year-old male on a multiple-hundred mile road trip, with his mom's vehicular baby, and gave him a credit card. This brings me back to the question, "Where did I lose control?"

I trust Paul. I have always trusted Paul, but there are some ideas that do seem, well . . . , a little foolish on face. To top everything else off, the kid has done very little driving over the last couple of years, and he certainly has never driven anything like his mom's Beethoven.

Susan and I made this same trip, in that same car a few months back, and well . . . er . . . ah . . . don't tell anybody in law enforcement . . . but on a flat stretch of desert interstate, out in the absolute, geographical center of nowhere, I surrendered to a seriously juvenile impulse and experienced speeds measured in three digits. If Paul's sedate, mature, reserved, intelligent, handsome, brave, clean and reverent daddy, can succumb to such evil enticings, how can a 21-year-old hope to remain in control?

In point of fact my concern about losing control is clearly misplaced.

With seven children, and six of them sons, I should have realized long ago that I began losing control the day the first wee widget took the spoon in his own hand and began shoveling mashed peas into his mouth without parental assistance.

Paul and Becca will survive, and the car—most likely—will be none the worse for wear. Even the abuse of the credit card will probably be limited, and I will pretend that I am sane and reasonable when I see them all again.

●　●　●　●

When Widgets Become Daddies

When the Saintly Susan and I first got into the baby business, the possibility that one of these wet, squirming, screaming things would one day have babies of his or her own never really registered.

Aaron, 25, our first born, grew up—something of a surprise in itself—got married, and promptly provided us with the three greatest grandchildren born on the planet to date. We were just getting used to this grandparent thing—all three of the midget widgets have the disquieting habit of referring to me as Grandpa Susan—when a miracle happened.

Our number three son, Jared, announced he was getting married. Jared, who just turned 22, is a great kid. You've just got to love him. He's gentle, pensive, thoughtful, spiritual and kind, but in a family noted for its weirdness, Jared was the unusual child.

If there was somebody likely to turn left while the rest of the world went right, it was going to be Jared. Jared didn't exactly march to the beat of a different drummer. He was more likely to skip.

Even as a young child, Jared was the kind of a person who would give you the shirt off his back or the bean he had just pushed up his nose. When he was about 6, the freckle-nosed widget with the big blue eyes and the unruly hair, disappeared entirely.

One morning, for no reason I can explain, Jared announced he was no longer Jared. He was now "The Credible Birdie." Where this bird came from I will never know, but its function was to "gaaaawwwwwwwkkkkkkkk" at every creature in sight. People in the store, strangers on the street, passing police officers and important telephone callers all got "gaaaawwwwwwwkkkkkkkked" without regard to station or status.

The Credible Birdie eventually vanished and in what seemed like a very short time, from a parent's I-don't-remember-getting-older perspective, a 6-foot, 3-inch man took his place.

The real miracle about Jared's marriage is the woman who loves him. At first blush there is no similarity between Jared and Stephanie except they both breathe air. Jared never wore pants that didn't have holes. Stephanie never owned anything that had a hole. Stephanie is organized and precise while Jared is random and scattered. It wasn't until we got to know Stephanie that we found out she is as pleasantly weird as is our Jared. During the couple of years since she has been an Aylworth, we've seen why the two are a match.

Last Christmas they exchanged a medieval battle axe and a two-handed broad sword as gifts. It is a good thing they love each other or such presents would make me worry.

About a month ago this couple announced that in May they will be adding an Aylworth to the clan.

The idea of Jared being a daddy, seems about as likely as the "credible birdie" becoming a man who goes to work each day, pays his bills, adores his charming wife, and still likes to play with his younger brothers. Nonetheless, Stephanie and the doctor both confirm that for the next few months she can refer to herself in the plural.

It will be fun to watch Jared be a father. I can predict his style will include endless amounts of love. The one thing I hope is Jared and Steph don't go ahead with their current plan to name the wee widget Kong.

Hmmm... "Come here, Kong. Climb up on Grandpa Susan's lap."
I suppose I could get used to it.

●　　●　　●　　●

An apology to my first born

Yesterday a truly shocking and disturbing event took place. Aaron, my firstborn, turned 28!

I have long felt I owed Aaron a public apology. As a firstborn he was faced with the twin challenges of growing up and dealing with an utterly untrained father. Aaron had it better than some because his dear mother, the saintly Susan, was the oldest of five children. As a result she had considerable practical experience with mini-widgets.

Good ol' dad, on the other hand, was the youngest of two, and to say I was clueless was to give me way too much credit. I had never diapered a baby before the day I bared his little bum for the first time.

Aaron had to teach me to be ready to duck when first exposing his little male parts to the open air. He also taught me the danger of bouncing a baby over my head just after he had eaten. Aaron taught me that animal crackers can be the difference between finishing the grocery shopping while still sane, and 20 minutes of screaming child. In the midst of truly abject poverty, this little boy taught me that 20 cents' worth of stale bread and a duck pond can generate more glee and giggles than tickets to Disneyland.

He taught me that courage, and even grace under pressure, doesn't require age or experience, when, as a tiny lad, he took time to thank the doctor for stitching up his tongue after a traffic accident.

Aaron proved to me the screaming, raging, rampaging, two-legged hormone, who is genuinely surprised I have adequate gray matter to breathe without assistance, is actually related to the little boy who used to sit on my lap. With his help, particularly during his mid-teen, young urban terrorist period, I learned the necessity for and value of prayer.

Aaron showed me that his being a crazy, raving wild thing didn't prevent his father from being even more stupid. He taught me that sincere, patient love is the greatest thing a parent can learn, and ultimately is the only thing that counts.

I've also learned what a father can feel seeing the man, husband and father his little boy has become. He's taught me that a deep, male voice saying, "I love you Dad," can bring just as many tears of joy as did a very little boy's voice saying, "I wuv you, Daddy."

He taught me things that have helped his younger siblings and he has taught me a whole lot more that has helped me to be a better man. So to Aaron I must say, "I'm sorry for every dumb thing I have done. I'm proud of the man, husband and father you have become, and most of all, I love you, son."

● ● ● ●

Everybody respects the wooden spoon

My darling bride, the saintly Susan, is gentle, warm, loving, hard working, nurturing to a fault, generous, and kind, but anybody fool enough to mess with this dear lady does so at his or her own peril.

It's not that Susan's sweetness is a veneer. She is in fact just as angelic as she appears, but 33 years of being married to me and nearly 32 years of mommyhood, have taught my dear bride that sweetness goes further when it is backed up with a great left hook.

I should say here Susan is not prone to physical violence. If she were I would very deservedly spend a lot of my time in an emergency room getting stitched up. It is also worth mentioning that it takes something more than a little over the top to provoke my girl. In point of fact, Susan reacts to even the most outrageous behavior by softly asking, "Now, how badly would you have to feel to act like that?"

Usually, she asks that at about the time I'm ready to drag some perceived miscreant backwards through a knot hole, and she is trying to keep me calm.

When our widgets were in or near the rug-rat stage, a deeply frustrated mommy would occasionally threaten to get out "THE WOODEN SPOON!"

I'm not sure any of the kids ever even saw the monster kitchen utensil, but they all knew it was nine and a half feet long and was covered with razor sharp hooks.

If she was slightly more incensed, then she would threaten to perform a "bottom-otomy" on the misbehaving child.

The fact all seven of ours still have their collective bottoms intact proves she never carried out any posterior removals, despite the threat.

As a rule of thumb it usually required a significant threat to the health, safety or personal reputation of one of our kids to set Susan free. When the widgets began producing grandwidgets, the umbrella of mother bear protection expanded to cover the new arrivals as well.

However, there are some behaviors that can ignite Susan's fire without a threat to her offspring, and one of the most certain to get things going is to lie to her.

Susan doesn't lie, period, and she has exactly zero tolerance for those who do. That came to the fore not long ago when she answered a television ad. A company was offering to give away, allegedly for free, some computer software.

Susan wanted some of the items that were being advertised and she called the 800 number to sign up.

From the moment she called I could tell she was . . . well . . . unhappy.

They wanted to get Susan to buy-up, and they pressed her. It was clear nobody wanted to just do what the ad had offered and my bride was mad about being lied to. Eventually she got off the phone, having made the order she wanted, but she was still smoldering.

The smoldering moved to open flame when the order arrived in the mail and still included things she didn't want and wasn't going to pay for.

Since she couldn't reach through the phone to throttle the salesperson, she reached for the keyboard. In a few well chosen words this gentle lady, all in the most controlled language, explained to the company why she felt the ground should open up and swallow their whole entire enterprise.

She, ever so sweetly, questioned their honesty, their ancestry, and their toilet training.

Susan explained there was no circumstance under heaven that would see her pay for anything she didn't order, and if they tried to bill her for such an item she was going to track down the appropriate legal jurisdiction and have the company well and truly abused in public. After sealing the letter in an asbestos envelope to protect the innocent, she launched the thing off to the company in question.

While the company never did strictly speaking apologize to Susan, they did send back a form letter saying there would be no future billings, and even refunded the money she had spent.

I suspect Susan wouldn't have actually damaged anybody at the company, even if they had ventured to within arm's reach, but she clearly did demonstrate even alleged grown-ups can perk up when the wooden spoon comes out.

●　●　●　●

Catsup snatcher to groom

Just when I think I have a minute to stop and smell the butterscotch, one of my widgets jumps up and slaps me upside the head with reality.

Matthew, nearly 23, has always attacked the world head on. When he had just mastered two-legged transportation he used to loiter around the refrigerator, waiting for an unwary soul to open the door. As soon as the door opened, the little raider would swoop in, grab the catsup, and run giggling toward the back of the house.

Just what his fascination was with this particular condiment was something none of us ever understood, but its capture was, for some months, the focus of his life. When not kidnapping the catsup, Matthew had a single goal in his just post toddler world, to be utterly miserable.

From the time he reached his second birthday until he was in his sixth or seventh year, we dubbed this little curly-haired angel with an attitude Miserable Matthew. He could be offended to distraction because the sun came up without his permission.

I remember with the sort of crystal clarity that only pain can etch into the human psyche coming to my happy home one afternoon to find the saintly Susan physically restraining herself from strangling her fourth-born son. For his part Matthew was screaming at the absolute top of his not inconsequential lungs.

Realizing this was a situation where a sane, sound, fatherly hand was needed, I asked Susan what in creation was wrong with the kid.

"I asked him to put on his shoes," she answered. She had made the request when the wailing widget first emerged shoeless from his bedroom just after dawn and announced his intention to go play in the backyard. Nine hours later, Matthew had yet to make it to the backyard, and was still protesting this outrageous request.

Thankfully, he outgrew Miserable Matthew and worked his way into Mighty Matthew. He became one of those people the angels loved.

I remember with fatherly pride watching him warm up for his first string slot on the varsity football team. Just before kick-off, he trotted to the sidelines and with his helmet tucked under this arm, he sang the National Anthem. The team went on to win the homecoming game and Matthew took one of the homecoming princesses to the victory ball. The kid lived everybody's high school fantasy.

For the most part Matthew hasn't been much of a problem in recent years. He's been at college out-of-state and when he wasn't there he spent a couple of years in Korea. The result is, except for a substantial impact on the pocketbook, Matthew has been a low maintenance child.

Last weekend he found a way to raise the family stress level. He flew home from college long enough to make his sweetheart his fiancée. Then the couple decided their marriage will be in 10 weeks.

With that Matthew hopped on a plane, headed back to college and left his fiancée, in-laws and parents to handle those little marriage details. Marie, his intended, is a dream-girl and if I didn't like her so well I would just disown Matthew and have done with it. But if we want to keep her, we have to keep him, and she is clearly worth the effort.

This means that for a few weeks we will all go mildly berserk to prepare for a wedding. It all proves the only constant in life is change and even Miserable Matthew grows up.

● ● ● ●

The Fine Art of Flirtation

Recently my 18-year-old son, John, has discovered a great hole in his universe of knowledge. He has no clue how to flirt.

Tall, handsome, an athlete, and the leader of his own rock band, you'd think John would be beating girls away with a stick. In fact he has no trouble meeting members of the opposite gender. They gather to him like moths to a warm, strong light, but he has no idea what to say after "Hello," and sometimes he can't get that right.

The other day, while riding his bike home from the local university where he goes to school, a young lovely risked life and limb cutting across three lanes of busy traffic to stop her bike next to his. A big smile and a warm, "Hello," got John's attention.

When the light changed the young lass playfully sped off on her bike with the unspoken challenge for John to catch up. John understands challenges, and with a burst of athletic splendor he peddled past the young beauty, and for good measure, flashed through a red light and rode for a block more. Then it hit him: He'd won the race and lost the contest.

Despite evidence to the contrary, John is frighteningly smart and he has had a series of truly lovely girlfriends, but these were young ladies with tenacity, who wouldn't take I'm-too-dumb-to-breathe as an answer.

With persistence they bore through John's natural inclination to be a social catastrophe, and discovered what John's family all knew. Beneath the carefully cultivated, "I-am-a-dumb-jock" persona that John wears like a dirty T-shirt, there is a really sharp guy. (He also scored way high on his SAT. John asked me to put that in so he wouldn't look like a moron.)

To make matters worse John has a younger brother who is a past master at flirtation. Paul is only 15 and "officially" he has never dated, but since he learned to walk he has always had a skill for meeting and then charming females of any age. Also tall, handsome, and athletic, Paul is one of those people who can say outrageous things to strangers and come off as endearing rather than stupid.

For his 12th birthday we had a party at a local skating rink. He invited half a dozen buddies but there was a striking lack of females. Paul fixed that by meeting, charming and inviting to the party a delightful blonde beauty two years his senior. The two are still friends and because she lives in a town 20 miles up the street, I have the phone bills to prove it.

Where John stammers and stumbles, Paul has a golden tongue. John has asked Paul for advice, but I think it really bothers him to be a college freshman getting tips on flirting from a high school sophomore.

John is trying. For one thing he has taken to planning and writing down "spontaneous" things to say to girls.

The poor kid has gone so far as to ask his ancient father for advice. As I remember, I was once pretty good at flirting, but that was back in the dark ages when if we wanted to pass notes in class we first had to scratch them onto a rock. Since I met the saintly Susan, I haven't had much need for flirting with anybody but her, and Susan loves me even when I'm a major jerk, a not entirely unheard of condition.

About the only thing I can tell John is to be what he really is, smile when he wants to smile, and just stop peddling his bike so fast.

● ● ● ●

My baby is headed for China

If all goes as planned, and I'm not entirely sure I want it to, in about six weeks my darling daughter is going to China.

At some level I suppose I should be used to the fact that my children are globe trotters.

I have had sons in Australia, Korea, and Venezuela for years at a time. Within the confines of the good old U.S. of A., I have had children living in Georgia, Louisiana, Texas and Utah at one time or another.

But there is something about China that just makes it all a little different, particularly when my baby girl, Rebecca, is concerned.

Becca is my youngest, and my only daughter, but by any reasonable definition she is an adult. She has also demonstrated a talent for dealing with a range of challenges. Just surviving six older brothers demonstrates a better than average sense of self-preservation. I've also seen her punch out at least two of her older siblings, when she thought it necessary.

However, this wonderful sense of personal empowerment and self-confidence has its own set of drawbacks. For one thing my Becca doesn't entirely understand there are times when being scared is a good thing.

A couple of years ago, when she found a bare-chested man rummaging around in her van, she didn't run for help. She didn't back off when the man said he was hiding from the police.

She ordered the miscreant out of her vehicle, demanded he return a sweat shirt—the only thing he found in the van worth stealing—and then she climbed into the van and drove off, leaving the startled fugitive standing in the parking lot.

About 20 minutes later, while running an errand in a nearby store, just what she had done finally got through to my baby girl. She dissolved into a puddle of tears and called dad to come get her.

Now, my baby wants to go the other side of the planet, to spend six months volunteering in a program that teaches English to small children. It's an honorable, almost noble endeavor, and just how I'm going to pay for it, I haven't a clue, but the point is she isn't just crossing a time zone or two.

My baby is going to be on the other side of the international dateline. We won't even be sharing the same day at the same time. And on top of everything else, it's China!

China was one of the boogie men countries of my youth. Red China was a bad place. I grew up in era of the 1965 hit the "Eve of Destruction," when singer Barry McGuire urged all of us teens to "think of all the hate there is in Red China" and Becca wants to go there to help make the world a better place. She will learn things I have never known and see the sun rising over one of the oldest nations on the globe.

She will come back speaking at least some Chinese, and she will come away from this—amazingly to her daddy—a better person than she was when she left.

As an intellectual issue, I know there is no reason to believe she won't be entirely safe. The group she is going with has lots of experience and she will be well protected and chaperoned, but she is my baby.

She'll be fine, but I may need six months worth of tranquilizers.

● ● ● ●

Roscoe and I miss daughter

I saw Roscoe crumpled in the corner, looking a whole lot more miserable than usual, which is frankly hard to imagine, but I understood his mood.

Roscoe is a stuffed dog toy. He might be a beagle or maybe a springer spaniel, I've never been entirely sure, but he is black and tan, with enormous floppy ears, curly soft-fuzz for hair, and mournful eyes.

This rather bedraggled ersatz canine joined the Aylworth household when my darling daughter, Rebecca, was hospitalized because of an emergency appendectomy.

My dear wife, the saintly Susan, and I were not going to be able to overnight in the hospital with our baby, and Becca looked so pathetic. In a moment of what might have been inspiration—it could also have been indigestion. I have a hard time telling the two apart— I grabbed this plush pup in a grocery store.

I presented the stuffed dog to Becca, who promptly cuddled up against him, and christened her new friend Roscoe. I had anticipated the critter might provide Becca a degree of contact comfort during her stay in the hospital. Somewhat to my shock, Roscoe became a permanent fixture in her life.

Roscoe slept on or in Becca's bed from that day onward. When she headed off to college, Roscoe was matriculated with her, too. None of my kids ever had a special blanket, or even a pacifier when they were of the right age.

Aaron, my oldest, when he was just out of the rug-rat stage, had a pair of imaginary friends, "Spin Indian" and "Macaroni Sauce," who lived under the table in the living room and ate candy canes from the Christmas tree.

However, even Spin and Macaroni were passing visitors.

Roscoe became my Becca's buddy, and he has held that role as she moved out of her teens and from girl to womanhood.

That's why when I found Roscoe abandoned in what had been Becca's bedroom, I was more than a bit startled.

My baby is in China, and she will be there for the next six months.

Sending my one and only daughter to the absolute other side of the planet has stressed my already fragile psyche, but through the magic of e-mail we have been in almost constant communications, and things have been just this side of horrible.

A public toilet on a back road in a poor suburb of Tijuana would look like a palace next to her apartment. The temperatures are cold enough to freeze dry a polar bear, and the only heat for the entire building comes from a lone space heater in Becca's living room, which, if nothing else, makes her apartment the most popular room in the complex.

At some level, the wicked little boy in me that would dip girls' pig-tails into inkwells, and put tacks on chairs, is rather amused by the living conditions. I mean I want her to look forward to coming home.

The daddy part of my soul, a part that Becca has very strong ties to, is well and truly anguished.

By her second or third electronic missive, Becca was sounding a bit more at ease. She and her roommate had scraped off the first couple of layers of scum and slime out of the apartment, a neighbor had fixed the bathroom door so it would finally close, and she was beginning to learn how to manipulate the toilet, which apparently has a mechanical aversion to disposing of toilet paper.

It was in response to the more positive note that I told Becca I had found Roscoe and he looked really lonely.

She wrote back and explained she simply could find no way to get the little guy into her already stuffed luggage, and had reluctantly decided to leave him home.

Then she advised me to give Roscoe a hug.

I did.

I think I may be the only person who misses Becca more than Roscoe, so I've decided to try to help him feel better. I wonder if Susan would mind if Roscoe slept in our bed, say for the next six months or so?

● ● ● ●

Parenting never ends, even if childhood does

I have no idea where it started—I know I'm not responsible— but there is this absurd myth that parenting ends when the widget in question attains the ripe old age of 18. All of my seven offspring have long ago reached and passed that magic year, but even so my daddy license has never expired.

Parents continue to be parents. What changes is widgets stop being kids. Without so much as asking permission, people who were crumb-grinding rugrats grow inexorably into full-sized humans. What's more, these enlarged children develop a sense of independence.

The point is, parents are still involved in parenting but the people who are the targets of that parenting become much less inclined to listen to the wise advice of their forbearers. In my clan this inclination to widget self-determination is nowhere more evident than in means of transportation.

From the moment my kids were old enough to understand speech, I set down a law when it came to means of locomotion. Motorcycles were forbidden.

I can hear the howls even now. "Motorcycles are as safe as the driver! They are fun to ride! They sip gas! They can be parked any-where!" I don't debate any of that. The other point that at least in my mind is beyond debate, is in any dispute between a four-wheeled rolling steel box and a two-wheeled vehicle, two wheels lose.

It doesn't make a whit's worth of difference who was in the right. It is a matter of physics. Mass times velocity equals all sorts of really unpleasant damage to the human body.

I suppose I should confess that I owned an anemic excuse for a motorcycle. I rode it all over town. I was very proud of the fact that this silly one-piston bike cost me about a nickel a mile to run.

After dumping the bike twice in six months, and breaking both collarbones, one in each crash, I came to the realization that with both collar bones gone, my neck was clearly in line for the next break. So I gave the motorcycle away.

The conviction that my little bike had tried its level best to kill me dead led to the edict from Mount Dad and that pronouncement was a source of enormous friction between some of my sons and me. Others, the more clever, never challenged me on this one. They just rode their buddies' bikes when they were out of my sight, but the line was drawn in the sand: Four wheels and no fewer! At least in terms of owning or overtly operating motorcycles, the paternal order was publicly honored.

Once they "grow up"—and I use that term with some hesitancy—then all bets are off. I know there are motorcycles and off-road vehicles of various flavors hiding in my kids' garages. But they aren't under my roof, and for some strange reason my grown-up widgets think they have a right to do what they want.

On the other hand, kids who think they understand old dad can misinterpret the house rules.

A couple of weeks back I got a call from my son, John. For the record John is an officially grown up married man who lives under his own roof.

"I know you're not going to like this Dad, but I'm getting my pilot's license."

To his surprise, I was thrilled. I have a whole long list of places I want to visit and a kid who can fly me there would be very handy. Also I know private planes are statistically among the safest ways to travel. But even if I was staunchly opposed, what could I do? Cancel his allowance? Order him to go to his room?

It is not that parenting ends. It is the capacity to enforce parental edicts that fades. I discovered a long time back that true parental power begins to disappear very early in the kid-dad relationship: Real control peaks the day before the little guy grabs the spoon in his own tiny fist and begins to shovel the mashed peas into his own mouth without help.

●　●　●　●

May you have a kid just like yourself!

With all of my widgets grown, married and gone, I have kids scattered randomly across the landscape like gopher holes in an ill-tended lawn.

From time to time they all check in with the old folks, but as a rule we hear from them less often when things are going well. That's part of how I knew there was a problem the instant I heard my senior son's voice on the phone.

He wasn't crying, or groaning, or anything like that, but there was something sort of bleak in Aaron's tone. "Dad, remember the curse?"

Of course I remember the curse! There came a day when Aaron was about 16 and deeply into his young urban terrorist period, when I held my right hand to heaven and solemnly intoned the great curse all parents know: "May you have a child just like yourself!"

I know, and adore, all three of Aaron's children. The kids are polite, patient and enthusiastic. Having said that, I've always harbored a suspicion that Aaron's eldest daughter, Samantha, 13, would be a great source of gray hair for my son. She is a beauty who is frighteningly intelligent, is learning to play the oboe, and has a definitely impish side to her personality.

"What did Sammie do?"

"It wasn't Sam, Dad. It was Austin."

Austin? Austin is 15 and, second only to his Grandma Susan, he is my top candidate for sainthood. He gets As in school. Does his homework without being prodded. Does his chores cheerfully, and rarely beats either of his two younger sisters. "What did Austin do?" I gasped.

It seems my oldest grandwidget is learning to drive and like many people in his age group, he believes that since he has ridden in a car all his life, he already knows how to operate one. His Mom,

Barbara, was trying to explain some of the finer points of navigating the road, like not running into stationary objects, and Austin responded, perhaps too forcefully, that he already knew all that stuff! He then promptly smashed his mother's pride-and-joy pickup into the family mailbox, doing $700 worth of damage to the truck and crushing the box.

To keep his batting average right where it was, he tried to blow the entire incident off as "no big deal."

When Aaron called me, Austin was in his Dad's shop under strict orders to return the battered mailbox to something approaching a usable condition. Aaron was also giving his son some time to worry about what would happen next.

My son asked, "Dad, what should I do?"

Aaron was making the understandable, if erroneous assumption, that since I had raised seven kids without a felony conviction in the lot, I must know something magical for a situation like this. I was still struggling with the concept that Austin could do something so utterly in-keeping with his age and mid-adolescent hormonal conditions.

Then I recalled a day, clear back in the last century, when then 16-year-old Aaron parked our family car under the rear bumper of a stopped Mustang.

It seems a particularly fetching teen lovely was strolling down the sidewalk, and Aaron was so captivated by her rear end that he didn't notice the rear end of the Mustang that was stopped for the light.

I honestly can't remember exactly how I responded to Aaron's vehicular misdemeanor. Since he is still alive, I clearly didn't act on my first impulse. The state of California proved to be an ally in this case, because it unceremoniously revoked my kid's driver's license, a decision I heartily applauded.

"Aaron," I said into the phone, "The first thing is you can't kill him because murder, no matter how justified, is socially unacceptable."

Then I suggested he give his son a hug, which will confuse Austin no end. I also recommended Aaron tell his son, "I'm really disappointed in you," which will hit harder than any punishment the boy might be imagining.

After I hung up, I realized that, as far as I can tell, my kids with widgets of their own, all have offspring just like themselves—and they should thank heaven every day for such wonderful blessings.

● ● ● ●

Widespread family offers chance for panic

With widgets spread from coast to coast, I generally look forward to phone calls from my kids, but this call from my senior son, Aaron, was an exception.

"Dad, I knew you would be worried about us, and I want you to know everything is fine," said Aaron to my answering "Hello." As a general rule I'm pleased to hear my kids are all happy and everything is wonderful in their lives, but this particular happiness report seemed to have a back story.

I had no idea why I was supposed to be worried, which is unusual for me because I can worry about whether the sun will come up on time.

"Jared (Aaron's brother who lives two doors down the road from him in a suburb of Atlanta) lost most of his fence and we had water in the basement."

Jared lost a fence? How does one "lose" a fence and why is their water in the basement?

"The carpet is pretty much ruined in Austin's room, but there was no major damage."

Austin is Aaron's 13-year-old son and the concept that the carpet in a 13-year-old boy's room could be ruined didn't come as a great big shock. Heck, when Aaron still lived in Casa Aylworth—clear back before the turn of the century—I can remember months at a time when I never saw Aaron's bedroom carpet because of the mounds of clothes and debris that covered it.

"Aaron, what exactly are you talking about?" I asked.

"The hurricane, dad, Hurricane Emily!" Aaron made the statement with this sort of "What's wrong with you? Have you been living under a rock?" tone in his voice.

In point of fact I had not been living under a rock. I visit under there from time to time, but it is not a place I call home. This was way back in July—long before a hurricane named Katrina would attain the status of a curse word for the rest of eternity.

At the time I was aware of Emily, but I was also aware that—unless somebody moved it—Atlanta is a whole long way from the ocean. Emily had done rude things to Florida and was on her way to raise insurance rates in the Caribbean, but Atlanta seemed outside her soggy path.

"Dad, Emily didn't get near us, but we got some gusty winds and 10 inches of rain last night," Aaron explained. Winds had done a "we're-not-in-Kansas-anymore" number on Jared's fences, and the rain had sloshed down Aaron's driveway and into Austin's room.

Aaron had called to assure me and his mother, the saintly Susan, that the Atlanta contingent of the family tree was soggy but unbowed. That is sort of a backhanded way to get good news, but I'll take good news where I can find it, and after finding my way to the same page as my senior widget, I thanked him and wished the Atlanta group well.

Jump ahead six weeks when Katrina comes rampaging ashore in the Mississippi delta. I wasn't even visiting under a rock this time and with the help of the National Weather Service and a computer terminal, I had tracked the storm as she came ashore. Right there on the computer screen was a satellite image showing one of the great spiral arms of this monster sweeping over Atlanta.

So I did what I do best. I panicked. We started calling our kids back there and to add to our anxiety nobody was answering the phone. The fact we were calling in the middle of the day when a busy family is out and about didn't dawn on me at the time. I was pretty much convinced the whole wing of the family had been washed into the Chattahoochee River, and no, I did not make up that name.

A couple of hours later, Sammie, Aaron's senior daughter, returned our call to tell her sweet grandmother that they got a "little" rain, but everything was fine.

I am wildly grateful that my widgets, widgets-in-law, and grand-widgets back there are all well and safe, but I also want something put in place that tells me when to panic and when to remain calm.

I seem to waste a lot of panic on events that don't deserve it, and miss ones where getting a little crazy would be entirely reasonable.

● ● ● ●

Learning the father of the bride's role

I've strolled through wildfires, reported about rock-throwing rioters, waded through icy flood waters, and once spent three hours in a closet-sized room with Charlie Manson. Over the years I've come to believe I do pretty well under pressure, but recent domestic events are forcing me to reconsider that obviously self-deluded belief.

My two youngest widgets, Paul and Becca, after quietly conspiring behind old dad's back, are getting married. No, not to each other! My family is weird, but not THAT kind of weird!

In fact, I am both astonished and pleased by the two prospective spouses my widgets have selected. Paul is marrying a young beauty named Carly Jackson. She is a remarkably lovely young woman, who is a concert quality oboist, intelligent, charming, and astonishingly, is inexplicably in love with my son.

Becca's intended is Jonathan Wright. Yes, my baby girl is going to marry "Mr. Wright," which by itself is just too cute to comprehend. Jonathan is tall, handsome, bright, and clearly brave. Any man who wants to marry my daughter, knowing she has six wildly protective older brothers and a father who is a certifiable lunatic, is by definition fearless. For me, the most remarkable thing about Jonathan is I can't bring myself to hate him. He is such a good guy, and is so clearly head-over-heels in love with my Becca, I just can't help but like him.

It is not the fact that these four are going to become two couples that I find fearful. While they are being married in a double ceremony out-of-state, they are going to share a reception here, and that's what is teaching me about my limitations.

Since the event is happening here, and this is Rebecca's home town, she and Carly agreed that Becca could make the local arrangements. Paul showed better judgment than his dad, when he decided to keep his mouth shut, but not me. I was foolish enough to think somebody—anybody—would be interested in my ideas. So fat, dumb and happy, I made recommendations on where to hold the reception and what the entertainment should be. I was even so boorish as to express some ideas on the wording and design of the invitations.

Becca pretty much treated my thoughts as the ravings of a delusional old man. It's not that my widgets don't love me. It has more to do with they see the way I decorate if left to my own devices, and they know I generally look like an unmade bed. My dear bride, the saintly Susan, took time to explain my proper function.

The father of the bride, I was advised, should look good in his tux at the reception and smile a lot. Susan, in the tone she reserves for small children and the feeble-minded, went on to explain lovingly that prior to the actual event, I should sit in the corner and keep my mouth shut.

At least now I have a clear idea of my responsibilities, but I do wish there was a TV in this corner. It's going to get sort of boring after a while.

● ● ● ●

Grand-Widgets!

Princesses

Sammi, my not-quite 3-year-old granddaughter, is a cherub with an attitude.

She is endowed with both a smile and a pout that would melt lead and in a pinch she has a right cross to match. I was bouncing this enchanting bundle of energy on my lap the other evening, when for no apparent reason, she reared back and popped me smartly on the right eye with her right hand.

When I complained—LOUDLY—that my angelic, blue-eyed darling, granddaughter had just punched me, she denied all charges unashamedly.

Looking her squarely in the eye, I said, "You did too punch me!"

In that particularly sweet tone females of all ages use for talking to small animals and conning male relatives, Sammi protested, "I didn't PUNCH you. I hitted you."

To prove her point, she promptly didn't punch me again in my left eye.

It is against this delicate backdrop that my new daughter-in-law, Stephanie, the incredible young woman who married my son, Jared, declared that she and Sammi were princesses.

Now at the very best Jared is an earl or a viscount or some such, but if my daughter-in-law wants to anoint herself and my granddaughter as royals, who am I to disagree.

The idea stuck with Sammi who was very pleased, but she also attacked this with a very Sammi brand of logic. If Aunt Steph is a princess and Sammi is a princess, and Aunt Stepi and Sammi are girls, then (ergo) all girls are princesses.

Things went smoothly until Sammi decided to share her discovery about girls and princesses with another young lass in her pre-school.

"You're a princess," Sammi assured her miniature colleague.

"No I'm not," protested the little widget. "I'm a angel. My daddy says!"

Confronted with this obviously ill-informed child, Sammi forged ahead, telling the little girl—at increasing volume and shrill tone—that she was indeed a princess and her daddy just hadn't gotten the memo.

The idea that daddy could be wrong about anything dissolved the little girl into tears and brought the pre-school staff running to the disaster.

I heard about this later and was glad Sammi hadn't tried to establish the rightness of her position by *not* punching the other widget in the eye.

For my part I think Steph is right. She and Sammi are princesses, but at the same time I'm willing to concede that some small children may be angels or even frogs.

● ● ● ●

Past and future joy of a mob of cousins

When my widgets were in the early and just post crumbgrinder stage, one of the greatest words in their limited language was "cousins."

Around the Casa Aylworth, nothing could inspire much more youthful glee—except maybe Christmas morning—than the announcement that "the cousins" were coming.

Though there were five siblings between my dear bride, the saintly Susan and me, the magic word "cousins" referred to the offspring of Susan's sister, Patricia, and her husband Dale.

Their five widgets were close enough in age to our seven to allow the kind of mayhem and cheerful blood-letting that only occurs within the confines of a loving extended family.

Everybody had a more or less counterpart, and the bigger ones always found ways to involve the smalls in their conspiracies.

I remember a day when we were visiting Pat and Dale, and the kids were involved in some sort of a mock battle. Sean, Pat and Dale's youngest, was a babe in arms who hadn't even reached the crawling stage, but he was given a specific role. My son, Jared, who was maybe eight at the time, explained to me that Sean was their "observation officer."

"He doesn't report much, but he observes really good," explained Jared with an entirely straight face.

Cousin love was never a barrier to widget warfare.

My darling daughter, Rebecca, and her cousin, Lauren, were, and remain among each other's closest friends, which of course means when they weren't playing angelically together, they were doing their level best to remove each other forcibly from the family gene pool.

These two decidedly girly-girls could get into fights that would daunt your average Marine drill instructor.

It reached a point where Becca's dad—who is clearly endowed with the wisdom of King Solomon—ordered the pair to scream "I LOVE YOU!!!" at the top of their lungs at each other any time they were fighting.

When they followed my sage counsel, which really wasn't all that often, they both collapsed in uncontrollable giggles before they could finish screaming their affection at one another.

While they all did love each other, it remained the case that having all 12 of the cousins in one place could make any alleged adult begin to wonder whether a lifetime of celibacy was such a bad thing.

My senior niece, Rachel, who is a budding actress, was in her younger years a combination of the little blonde moppet from Alice in Wonderland, and the kid from the "Bad Seed." There were times when I was convinced Rachel would ultimately be named the "child most likely to grow up to be an axe-murderer."

At that point in her maturation, Rachel could justify even the most outrageous behavior by smiling sweetly and announcing, "My mommy said . . ." and then filling in the blank with anything from permission to live on a diet of animal crackers and peppermint ice cream, to playing jacks in the middle of Interstate-5.

Now, most of a generation further down the road, "the cousins" are the widgets of my widgets.

Until Jared, now a married man himself, with a son, Tanis, moved his portion of the clan three time zones east, his boy, and my son, Adam's firstborn, Anthen, were functionally joined at the hip.

Where one was the other was coming soon, and they couldn't have been much more like brothers without sharing the same parents.

This means periods of hugs and cheerful play were interspersed with intense, if fairly inept, fist fights, which then ended with giggles as often as not.

Sydnie, Adam's daughter, is clearly convinced her uncle, my son Matthew, and his lovely bride, Marie, brought their son, Jacob, into the world strictly as a live baby-doll for her amusement.

It is a joy to watch Sydnie, who just recently mastered two-legged ambulation herself, toddle up to her infant cousin and, as delicately as a 2-year-old can, gently cuddle little Jake.

For his part, Jacob responds to this affectionate assault with a wide, drooling, five-tooth grin.

The original "the cousins," have yet to generate any offspring— but Pat and Dale's senior son, Marcus, and his wife, Erin, have just announced that their clan will be expanding in about seven months.

I foresee a day when the widgets of the cousins, on both sides of the family, will look forward to opportunities to play with—or beat the poop out of—the second cousins or first cousins once removed or some such.

The title of the relationship won't be as important as the love and expanded family ties that grow far after this old fat grandpa will have shucked off this mortal form.

● ● ● ●

Never let sanity interfere with political correctness

About two years ago my good son, Jared, with his family, moved three time zones east. I know all the good reasons why he, his charming bride, Stephanie, and their outstanding son, Tanis, moved, but that doesn't mean I have been entirely comfortable with the relocation.

Being totally candid, I've especially missed Tanis. I met him the day he was born and I had a small part in watching and helping the little guy grow.

When he wasn't out in the yard—hunting "giggle-monsters" with his dear, sweet grandmother, my bride, the saintly Susan—he was in the house reading books, building blocks, or playing video games with his old fat grandpa.

Tanis was—and I am sure remains—a genuinely fun little widget, but now he has gone to the land eastward.

When he was physically close by, I took some grandfatherly pride in being one of Tanis' protectors. Bullies, beetles, spiders, overly aggressive kittens, and giggle monsters all knew they had to get through this grandpa before they could threaten my Tanis.

Now that he is on the other side of the continent, I can't be there to help Jared and Stephanie protect my glorious grandwidget from all enemies foreign and domestic. This concern for the little guy's well-being was sparked by a recent e-mail from Stephanie.

When it comes to physical protection from miniature miscreants of roughly his own age, I suspect Tanis is being well prepared. The little guy has a "junior yellow belt" in Tae Kwon Do. In point of fact

I don't have so much as a clue as to what that really means, but it sounds impressive, and the idea of my grandson kicking, chopping, punching and stomping around some karate dojo amuses me no end.

However, as it happens, most of life's challenges don't come at you kicking and punching. Tanis and his mommy got a taste of that when they both went a round with political correctness.

The little guy came home from school with an assignment to find a photo in a magazine that represented something starting with the letter "M." Tanis' parents are a hardworking young couple, who at this point don't have a lot of time or cash to devote to a wide library of magazines, but since Jared and Stephanie were first married they have shared an interest in medieval weapons.

They don't beat each other—or Tanis for that matter—with broad swords or morning stars, but they are intrigued with the weapons, have collected a few, and their sole magazine subscription is to a publication on the subject.

So with that lone magazine in the house, Stephanie dutifully helped Tanis go through the pages until they found an "M" object, a machete. Thinking she had succeeded in her motherly duties, she trundled her son off to school with his "M" clipping clutched in his hot little hand.

That's when the trouble began.

At Tanis' school "M" can stand for mouse, monster, marbles, madness, or mindless mischief, but it can't stand for machete, because machetes are weapons and the school has a strict policy against bringing weapons to campus, even if they are just a picture on paper.

This highly incensed teacher publicly chastised Tanis for being so confused as to do what she told him to do, and sent him home with a message "to tell his mother that the principal did not allow weapons of any kind at the school," according to Stephanie's e-mail.

I could understand the uproar if he had brought a real machete to class—even though I am pretty well convinced the other kids would have thought it "way cool"—but what is the danger of a magazine clipping?

The only way that clipping could have been considered a weapon was if Tanis had chewed it up and fired it across the room as a spitwad, and even that would have been more messy than dangerous. But I'm trying to respond to craziness with logic and that is always a hopeless endeavor.

Tanis, I'm sorry your teacher has lost her mind. I'm even more sorry she doesn't realize she is a nut case, but I'm afraid hers is a sort of craziness that is loose in the land, and you're going to have to deal with this one all by yourself.

● ● ● ●

Angels and miracles arrive together

A pair of miracles, appropriately accompanied by a pair of angels, were bestowed on the extended Aylworth clan last week. Miracles, and even visiting angels, aren't all that rare around this family. After all with my dear bride, the saintly Susan, as the chief cornerstone of the clan, gifts from a kindly Providence are almost a scheduled occurrence. In this particular case the angels and the miracles arrived two hours apart.

At about 7:30 p.m. April 14, Allie Mae, the daughter of my son Adam and his dear bride Dana, made a slightly ahead of schedule arrival in the old hometown.

Two hours later, and 500 miles to the north, Elise Rose, the daughter of my son Matthew and his lovely wife Marie, made her scheduled entrance into the world.

All babies are miracles, and all daughters are angels. As the father of six sons and a lone daughter, I'll grudgingly admit the male new arrivals can be pretty angelic too, but somehow the heavenly glow seems to linger longer with the female half of the population.

According to Susan, and I don't debate things celestial with my bride, Elise Rose arrived a little later than her twin cousin because she wanted to escort Allie Mae in for a landing, and Allie needed a little help.

While Elise is perfect as well as being . . . well . . . perfect, Allie is perfect but a bit damaged.

We have known for some time Allie's arrival would not be without challenge, and she is living up to her expectations. She has been moved to a special hospital where they take care of ailing angels.

Adam and Dana, along with Dana's parents Richard and Pattie, Susan and me, and just about every other member of both clans on this side of the planet, have made a pilgrimage to the hospital to touch, and see, and encourage our little angel to make earth her permanent address for the next eight or 10 decades.

She's still considering her options, but each day she stays adds to the likelihood she will decide to grace us with her long-term presence.

At the other end of the family, Matt, Marie, and Elise are home.

Matt's firstborn, Jacob, who has suddenly been elevated to the status of a "big brother" at the ripe old age of 2, is reportedly fascinated with his baby sister.

While Jake is way short of mastering the wonders of speech, when Elise cries he has no trouble telling his parents they had better get things fixed . . . right now! Elise is to be kept smiling and anybody who fails in that goal will to have to answer to her big brother.

Adam's senior child, Anthen, at 5, is an experienced big brother, thanks to not quite 3-year-old Sydnie.

This is Sydnie's first opportunity to be a big sister, and she is exploring the new role. Both are excited about Allie's arrival and, while the smells, sights, and sounds at the hospital are a bit distracting, they both want to spend as much time as they are allowed with "their" baby.

For my part, I'm deeply grateful these two angels have joined the clan. I'm spending a substantial amount of time asking The Boss to let Allie make her visit permanent, but the length of stay won't change how much any of them is loved.

● ● ● ●

Caden's arrival adds to grandwidgets

The "Moose" has landed!

I should make the point right off that my son, Adam, came up with the colorful nickname for his newborn son, but in all fairness it fits.

Just about 7:55 p.m. Sept. 9, Caden Andrew Aylworth took his first gulp of free air. Since that minute everybody who has seen the "little" tike, particularly those of the female persuasion, have had pretty much the same response:

"OH MY GOSH!"

Let me interject here that Caden is beautiful. In fact he looks very much like his daddy, and he's perfect in every way. The exclamation comes not from his appearance, but from his size.

Caden weighed 12 pounds at birth. No that is not a typo. That's 12, as in 10 plus two. Based on the premise that an 8-pounder is a big baby, my latest grandwidget is a baby and a half.

My dear daughter-in-law, Dana, Adam's amazing wife, has had big babies in the past, but there is big and then there is defensive tackle. After half a day of trying in the traditional way, Caden finally arrived when doctors provided him with an auxiliary exit and "POP," the Moose appeared.

Caden is the 10th grandwidget in our family group and the fourth child born to Dana and Adam.

During a hot summer, Dana patiently struggled through the last weeks of pregnancy, while continuing to juggle the demands of her own senior children, taking care of a house and being a wife to my son. None of that is easy, but Dana does it with such serenity and grace she makes it all look effortless.

I know this will come as a shock to some, but I have never been pregnant.

However, with seven kids of my own and now 10 grandchildren, I have closely observed the process with awe and wonder.

At the best of times giving birth is amazing.

I was present when five of my seven erupted into the world. The last two—like Caden—arrived by emergency belly zippers. I was unceremoniously ushered out of the room before they made a landing.

I don't remember my own birth—it was, after all, a very long time ago—but from what I can see, the process of reaching the outside world is no easier for the widget in transit than it is for the mom.

They are in a place that is warm, safe and secure. The scenery might not be much to shout about, but there is the reassuring sound of mom's heart beat and, if they are blessed, as mine have been, they can hear the music of their mother's laughter as well.

They have everything they need and since their experience with choice is fairly limited, they also have what they want.

Then all of a sudden forces they can't possibly understand grab these poor little angels and force them through a knot hole to emerge into a room full of bright lights, disturbing sounds, and people all wearing masks.

That would be more than enough to disquiet anybody.

Then strangers thump on the little one's feet to—of all things—encourage them to cry! Without any preliminaries they experience cold, hunger, and a whole lot more open space than they had any reason to believe existed. Once they're out in the world a parade of people, including me, want to touch them, bounce them, tickle them and generally add to the wee babe's discomfort.

Frankly it's a wonder any of us ever grow up.

Caden comes to the world as a very blessed child. He arrives with two of the most loving, dedicated parents I know. He also arrives with an older brother and sister, Anthen and Sydnie respectively, who sincerely want to love and care for him.

I like to think the last person to say good-bye to Caden before he came to this world was his other sister, Allie Mae, who returned to heaven too soon after visiting us here.

I look forward to getting to know Caden, to see his smile, and hear his giggle, and to see him glory in the family he has joined.

● ● ● ●

Diaper disaster surrenders to Brut force

Life is populated with a collection of times when things simply must follow a perfect script, and a recent summit of future in-laws just had to be one of them, but nobody told Caden.

John, our lone single son, in clear demonstration of his wisdom, intelligence, good judgment, and inexplicable good luck, fell in love with the amazing Amy. My dear bride, the saintly Susan, and I would be hard pressed to be more thrilled with John's choice.

We've had her in our home many times and have been consistently astonished at John's good fortune, but up until last week we had had only one brief, "hi and good-bye" opportunity to meet her mother Jean, and had never met her dad, Rob.

In an official and legal sense, there is no connection between the parents of the bride and the parents of the groom. However, in the process of marrying off six of our own widgets, we have come to realize there is a genuine need for a relationship between the future in-laws. Each of us is contributing a precious child to this union, and somewhere down the matrimonial road, both couples will be the ancestors of some extraordinary grandwidgets. All of that means it is somewhere between wildly important and ragingly necessary that Susan and I forge a positive relationship with Amy's folks.

When it comes to making a good first impression, I have no worries about my Susan. This lady can charm a rampaging flood if necessary, but first impressions are not always my strong suit. So when the morning of the "summit meeting" arrived, I made a point of not dressing in the dark, which is where I usually do my clothing selections. I picked out my best purple shirt and black slacks, and a tie I knew went well with the combo because Susan had told me they were complimentary. As long as you weren't looking too closely, or being particularly critical, I was looking pretty good.

Scheduling around my house is always a little hectic so, on the night of "THE DINNER" we also had our first chance to see Anthen, our 7-year-old grandwidget, play in one of his first baseball games. Since the game and the summit didn't overlap, we jumped on the happy opportunity to see Anthen play. Beyond the sheer joy of watching a collection of mini-baseball players abuse the national pastime, Susan and I would also have a chance to see Anthen's little sister, Sydnie, and their baby brother, Caden.

I arrived at the game before Susan and decided to exercise the grandfatherly prerogative of sweeping little Caden into my arms. Snuggled against my right side, the squirming little bundle of drooly-faced smiles was giving his grandpa an entire load of warm fuzzies. Unfortunately he was also depositing a load of an entirely different sort down the side of my shirt. A veritable stream of malodorous yellow-brown goo washed over my right side.

Dana, Caden's dear mom, discovered the disaster at about the time I began to wonder if a nearby septic tank was overflowing. She got some "wipes" to help clean my shirt, but while the stain pretty much vanished, the fragrance lingered. I'm no gourmet, but I was pretty sure essence of Port-a-Potty was not going to go well with dinner, particularly not for an in-law summit.

After the game ended in a tie—as I get it all the games in this league end in ties—Susan and I dashed home, where I stripped off the offended and offending clothing, gave my side a quick pass with a wash cloth, and drenched myself in enough Brut to smother the smell of a rendering plant.

With that, we took off to the restaurant.

I suppose the Brut worked, or maybe Rob and Jean were just too gracious to take official notice that I smelled like a teen-age boy's bedroom on prom night. However it worked, the wedding is still on, and Amy reported her folks really liked us.

I wonder if the inability to smell runs in their family? Oh well, who cares!

● ● ● ●

Senior grandwidget becomes teenager

I'm facing one of those moments where grandfatherly pride wars with a profound desire to deny my own advancing years. My senior grandwidget turns 13 this month.

The idea that Austin is 13 is not nearly so disturbing as the realization that I am old enough to have a 13-year-old grandson. If Austin's impending leap into the teens is disquieting to me, I have a hunch it is just short of overwhelming to the boy's dad.

Aaron is my firstborn, and I could not be prouder of him. In the nearly 15 years since he had the genuinely good sense and good fortune to marry the lovely and intelligent Barbara, Aaron has proven himself a loving husband, a dedicated daddy, and a surprisingly successful businessman. He has a lovely house and besides Austin, he has two beautiful daughters, Samantha and Alexis.

If Aaron trembles just a little bit at the thought of his eldest becoming a teenager, it may be because of his own history. Aaron was a cute little boy who as a toddler liked to have his tongue stroked, and was a great fan of walking trips to a nearby park where we could "feed-da-ducks-daddy!" Then about the time he hit his mid-teens, the charming lad disappeared one night and was replaced by a raging collection of hormones and adolescent angst. I call it his "young urban terrorist" period, and a goodly portion of the gray hair that now resides atop my scalp can be traced directly to those years.

Sanity pretty much ceased to be part of his world. Just saying "Good morning" could be interpreted as an utterly intolerable challenge to his masculinity and all he held sacred. Aaron emanated an attitude that would have prompted Mother Teresa to punch him out.

In the midst of all this, two things happened. He met Barbara, who, with a gentle touch and a willingness to smack him upside the head if needed, brought our firstborn back to his senses. The other event that took place, and I think might now be haunting my boy, was the father's curse I laid on him: "May you have a child just like yourself!"

I know it was a cruel thing to do, but I have to plead temporary insanity. Like they say, insanity is inherited. You get it from your kids. So now Aaron looks across the dinner table at Austin and wonders, "Are you the one?"

I personally don't think Aaron has anything to worry about with this boy. Austin is a kid who gets high grades, is excited about playing trumpet in the honor band, and is looking forward to becoming a cross country runner in high school.

Oh, I'm sure Austin will find ways to provide his dad with some gray hair, but I don't think this young man will ever ascend to his poppa's level of crazy-making. Sammie and Alex could be another story, but for entirely different reasons.

Aaron's two daughters are beautiful and smart. Since they are growing up in Georgia the two are developing honey-sweet southern accents which by definition can turn most men into puddles of goo. On top of that, their parents have helped these two develop a healthy sense of self-confidence and personal worth.

They already know how to wheedle daddy into doing just about anything they want, and when these two get dating-high, I suspect they are going to make a lot of males, including good ol' dad, more than a little crazy.

It will be fun to watch. I do love grandfatherhood.

● ● ● ●

Breaking the rules teaches lessons

When wee-widgets are at the toddler stage they have the utterly unshakable opinion that the big people in their lives are the ultimate authority on all things important.

In a few years—sometime around their 13th birthdays—they come to realize parents are clearly the dumbest creatures on the planet, and they pretty well hold to that opinion until they become parents themselves. Yet at the crumbgrinder stage they give us unreasonable credit for intelligence, and this blind faith can lead to some serious conundrums.

I had this point driven home recently when I watched a pretty young mommy and her curly-headed toddler. Mom was walking along a street that was closed to all but foot-traffic, and everything was perfect bliss until she brazenly stepped off the sidewalk and strolled into the middle of the road. The poor little guy obviously figured mom's trolley had completely bounced off the rails.

It was clear by the way he toddled right up to the very edge of the curb and came to a screeching halt, that long and sometimes diaper-paddling experience had shown him bad things happen if you run into the street. Then here was mom, not only violating one of the immutable laws of life and nature, but she was trying to entice him into doing something that could lead to his bottom hurting.

All this time Mom is standing in the center of the road calling and gesturing to her little darling, trying to encourage him to do something he knew full well he was not supposed to do. Finally, exasperated with her balky son, Mom returned to the curb, snatched him into her arms, and scolded him for being disobedient. This little guy could not have been more befuddled if Mom had sprouted a second head and started spouting split pea soup at passersby.

If being encouraged by Mom to do something "wrong" is confusing, having people ignore your magic words is equally frustrating.

My youngest grandson, Jacob, is a truly delightful 2-year-old with a throaty giggle and a smile that would melt any grandpa into a puddle of goo. Over his years, both of them, Jake has learned he can get just about anything he wants from his parents, my son Matthew and his glorious spouse, Marie, with the right approach.

If Jacob wants a glass of water, a taste of dad's ice cream, or some more Fruit Loops, he cups his two little hands in front of him and with one of his patented 10-megawatt grins, looks at the parent in question and says "Please?" which in Jacobese comes out "Peeze?" For Jacob, being killer cute and the word "peeze" were the answer to all life's requirements.

My dear bride, the saintly Susan, and I were visiting Jacob and his parents, and like good grandparents throughout time, we intended to spoil our grandwidget as much as possible. With that in mind, we took everybody to the park and the merry-go-round. Some clever marketer designed things so to get to the ride you had to walk through a small toy and gift store.

Going in Jake was too fascinated with the prospect of a merry-go-round ride to see anything else, but on the way out he saw it, a six-foot-tall, black plush, stuffed gorilla. Jake was transfixed. Except for arrowroot cookies and playing horsy with his daddy, this gorilla was the most wonderful thing he ever saw. Instantly Jake turned to his daddy, hands in cupping position, and said "Peeze?"

Matthew, either deliberately or by well-timed accident, missed his son's plea. To the empty air Jacob said "Peeze" one more time, then the little widget stared at his hands with this, "What went wrong?" look on his face.

I grabbed the little guy, stuck a nickel lollipop in his mouth, and tickled him until a torrent of giggles gurgled out around the candy, but I fear his faith in the power of the magic "peeze" was permanently shaken.

Learning that rules can be ignored under some conditions is one thing that comes with time and experience. Learning the world can ignore you, even if you say "peeze," is a continuing experience.

●　●　●　●

Here's living proof the head is mightier than the lip

To me, the darn thing feels like it enters a room 30 seconds before the rest of me arrives and, while that isn't true, I still have to admit my lower lip is kind of impressive.

The left side of my lower lip is split, bloodied, and a truly amazing shade of purple. This Technicolor ouchie sitting on the front of my face is hard to ignore, yet I find most people stare but don't ask.

The fact of the matter is I got beat up—smacked right in the chops—head-butted, to be brutally precise.

My dear bride, the saintly Susan, was there when it happened.

As she watched the tears pour down my cheeks and blood dribble over my chin, she started to say the obvious. "Oh baby, I think that is bad enough, you might need to go to the . . ."

I stopped her right there. "Nope! I'm not going to the hospital. There is no way in creation that I am going to explain how this happened to some doctor. I mean, do you really think anybody would believe this story?"

Although still lovingly concerned, Susan understood. How do I tell somebody that I got bashed and bloodied by my darling 6-year-old granddaughter?

We were visiting my son John's home. It was a minor family gathering. Besides Susan and me, and John and his wonderful wife, Amy, our older son, Adam, his glorious spouse, Dana, and their kids were all coming. Adam's senior daughter, Sydnie, is one of the primary joys of my grandparenthood, and what's more, she likes me too.

I was sitting at John's dinner table when dear Sydnie exploded into the room, dashed toward me, leaped into the air, executing a near-perfect half turn in space as she prepared to land backward on old Grandpa's lap. The problem was I hadn't anticipated this particular gymnastic maneuver, and I was leaning down to get her as she bounced up to me. The resulting collision brought the back of her pretty blonde head into lip-ripping contact with Grandpa's mouth.

Sydnie would never even consider voluntarily smacking Grandpa around, and the sight of my injury sent the little darling into heartbroken sobs as she hid behind her mommy, who was standing on the other side of the table holding Sydnie's new baby brother, Dallin.

So here I was on one side of the table crying and bleeding, Sydnie was weeping on the other side, and Adam sat between us laughing so hard he nearly passed out. Susan for her part was trying to soothe Sydnie, while making a largely unsuccessful effort not to laugh at me.

After a liberal application of ice, and a pile of bloodied paper towels, I was no longer actively bleeding and Sydnie was cuddled safely into my lap, after being convinced that Grandpa wasn't going to hate her forever.

Days later I still have this constant reminder that the head is mightier than the lip.

A few brave people have asked me what happened. One woman I know looked at me and said I looked like I had taken a well-placed right cross. I can't disagree with that. For my part I feel a bit like Rocky Balboa, in that I have vivid evidence I can successfully block a blow with my face.

I just wish I had a better story to go along with the war wound. I would much prefer to be able to regale friends and strangers with the tale of the titanic struggle between me and the mugger, or how I was hit in the face by the truck while dragging the adorable puppy out of the road. Almost anything would be better than to admit the truth on this one.

I suppose I could point out my "attacker" was a karate expert, which has the advantage of being semi-true. Despite her diminutive stature and tender years, Sydnie is a karate student with a purple belt. Yet the lip decoration will fade. Sydnie still loves me and, oh boy, will I have a cautionary tale to tell the young man who takes her on her first date.

● ● ● ●

Getting Fit

Body Warranty Expires

I woke up the other morning with the sudden realization that my body's warranty must have run out. Parts of me that hadn't even reported in for inspection in years suddenly hurt—and nothing was working up to the standard described in the owner's manual.

I think at least part of the problem is psychological. Paul, my youngest of six sons and just barely 15 years old, spent most of last year announcing he was "just about" as tall as dad. In the intervening months we rapidly passed "just about" and soared to "way taller" than dad. Having my "baby boy" look down at me from his lofty 6-foot-2 and pat me on the head is somehow disquieting.

This has also been the year that another family tradition has bitten the dust.

From the time the entire herd of widgets were genuinely little guys, I celebrated their birthday morning by hoisting them up in the air and banging their little noggins on the ceiling. By way of tradition and mutual consent this tradition ended with a kid's 16th birthday. The kids always protested, but I am convinced at some level they got a certain charge out of the roof rap.

When Paul turned 15, tradition demanded I hoist his manly form skyward for one last time, but there was no way I was going to be able to make this tradition fly. I quietly let it just slip, thinking Paul wouldn't notice. I thought I had gotten away with it until at dinner Paul announced dad must not love him anymore because the roof ride never materialized.

I would like to say it's the miles and not the years that sent this tradition to the showers, but the reality is . . . it's the years. I never officially admitted slipping from youth into middle age. It came as a shock recently that I could be halfway through my life and officially middle aged now—as long as I live to at least 95.

Years have their place. It takes time to accumulate as many great widgets, not to mention three super grandwidgets, as I have. I could not have been blessed with 26 1/2 years with the saintly Susan without the years passing.

Even so, a bit of youth is worth fighting for.

When I get home tonight I'm going to pick up the cat and gently bounce his head off the ceiling. Spats will have no idea what I'm doing, but at least I'll feel better.

● ● ● ●

One More Mountain to Climb

When I'm scared I won't be able to accomplish a goal, I tend not to tell anybody about the goal in the first place.

If I am all but certain that I can't do something and pretty sure I'll chicken out if I get half a chance, then I tell everybody I know what I have planned. That's what happened with my mountain climbing trip.

With the big 5-0—spell that fifty, as in half a century, the ancient of days—crashing in on me, I simply had to do something stupid, so I decided to climb a mountain.

The fact that I look like a relatively short, but fairly stout mountain myself, wasn't going to deter me from making an assault on this peak for my birthday. This is a 14,400-foot-high, darned near vertical mountain. Strong, healthy, young men and women tremble at the mention of its name as a climbing target.

To their credit my friends and co-workers did not immediately burst into hysterical laughter when they heard my plan.

Some may have snickered a little out of my sight and that can be forgiven, but several asked serious, concerned questions.

Have you really thought this through?

Have you considered some safer silliness, like Russian Roulette?

Do you have a fever?

Is your insurance paid up?

Even the saintly Susan, who is more or less used to my occasional bursts of insanity, was a little shocked by this particular stunt.

Initially I planned on going alone. I rather liked the idea of being the lone man challenging the mountain, and if I chickened out I could slink away with my tail between my legs and nobody would be the wiser. But Susan threatened me with permanent and painful, wife-inflicted, physical disability if I even thought about a solo journey and naturally I could see the reason in her argument.

So I invited my son, Jared, and a dear friend, Scott, to join me on my quest. I drove to the mountain weeks before the planned climb just to look at it. This sucker scared the pudding out of me.

I also took some pictures of the peak, which I kept on my desk.

I tried to convince myself the pictures were there for inspiration, but the fact was they were there strictly for the terror they generated.

On the day of the climb I knew I was in trouble the moment my boot hit the mountainside. With a pack on my back that was heavier than most compact cars, I began to trudge up the stony slope. Scott and Jared walked behind me and just sort of watched.

I think they both expected me to gasp and crumble to the trail at any minute, but death was never my primary fear. Dying on the mountain would have been inconvenient. I admit that, and I suspect Susan would have been seriously miffed at me, but it was humiliation, not visiting my long dead relatives, that really scared me.

Everybody I know and a bunch of people who won't admit to knowing me, knew I was doing this crazy stunt. I trudged along, head down and gasping for breath for a while, stopping every 10 or 15 feet for a five-minute break.

It wasn't long before it became abundantly clear: the mountain was going to win this round. I had no more chance of getting to the top, or the middle for that matter, than I did of sprouting wings and flying around the overwhelming pile of stone. With success out of the question, I began wondering what constituted failure. While I had certainly hoped to put in a better showing, I had never truly expected to reach the top. It was the trying that was important.

Well, I had tried, and I found out just how much more preparation I need to make a better showing in the future. When I gave up and turned my back on the mountain, it was tough. Ego, particularly one's own ego, is a very painful thing to trample on, but I'm not willing to concede defeat.

Now I know what I need to do and come next June I'm going back up that peak. Jared and Scott have already signed on for Crazy Climb Two, and a third friend, Steve, says he wants to join the band.

While the assault will again be on the mountain, the real contest is against myself, and no mountain, no matter how high, presents a bigger challenge than that.

● ● ● ●

Dying Loomed as an Acceptable Option

After about 10 miles I was pretty sure I was going to die, and under the circumstances that was a fairly attractive option.

It started, as most of my spectacularly stupid stunts do, as an attempt to do something healthy. Last July I made a near-fatal attempt to climb a 14,500-foot-high mountain, as a monument to my 50th birthday. I was so utterly humiliated by that failure that I vowed to really climb the peak before my next natal date, which meant I had to get healthier.

Over the last few months I have walked more treadmill-miles, pumped more iron, and generally labored more diligently than any time in recent memory, and I have made some progress.

My pants are less tight, my wind much improved, and I no longer break into a sweat walking from the couch to the kitchen, but working out in the gym and accomplishing my mountain-high goal are different.

With that in mind, I decided to walk the 12.5 miles to a neighboring foothill—as in all uphill—community.

Since my dear wife, the saintly Susan, was out of town, and I hadn't mentioned the idea to her before she left, there was no one to object to my insanity.

I got one of my sons to drop me off at my selected starting point and arranged—I thought—with my kids to be home for a cell phone call when I finished my hike.

The first few miles were actually pleasant. I just walked along, singing to myself—probably terrifying any wildland critters within earshot—and generally feeling smug about my glow of glorious health.

By the time I had crossed the eight-mile mark, that glow had faded to a weak glimmer, and half-a-dozen buzzards began circling overhead.

I'm sure they thought a very large meal couldn't be more than a few steps away.

Over the next two miles, the prospect of lying down by the roadside and gasping out my last breath did have its appeal. Only one factor kept me upright and plodding, pride.

I could live with dying, but failing—again—in front of my children would be too much to bear.

It crossed my mind that I could hitchhike to my destination, but I was sure my kids would look into my eyes and know I had cheated, so I plodded.

The last two miles were a grinding uphill struggle, but to my surprise I made it. There I was! My Little Engine that Might had prevailed. My day was made, until I made my cell phone call.

When the answering machine came on, I was sure the kids were going to be home in minutes, but when I called a few minutes later, I got to talk to the machine again and this conversation wasn't any more enlightening.

I vowed to call every 15 minutes until I made contact with my loving, if misplaced, off-spring.

John, my 21-year-old son and senior widget in residence, later told me I violated that vow and called about nine times in the next 20 minutes.

After the calls home resulted in nothing but added chats with the answering machine, I called one of my married sons, Jared, and begged him to collect his pathetic paternal unit, which, given the choice of listening to me whine, he agreed to do. Then I called the old homestead one more time to tell that end of the family not to come for me because I had arranged an option.

About 20 minutes, or three years later—desperation does tend to stretch one's relative time sense—to my surprise, John pulled up. He explained he had walked in about the time I hung up from my last call and he phoned Jared to say he would make the poppa pickup.

My kids—who are always convinced that dad is at least half nuts—were frankly amazed I made it, and so was I, but my real question was why I ever decided to try.

● ● ● ●

No heavier burden than raised expectations

Saturday morning was beautiful. The sun was shining, temperatures pleasant, and I was pretty sure I was out of my mind.

For the fourth or fifth year in a row, I was standing at the starting line, preparing to drag my overweight, under-exercised, gray-headed body over 13-plus miles of pavement, for no better reason than to prove I could. Last Saturday was the annual running of the Bidwell Classic Half Marathon, and just as if I had good sense, I was there with about 1,200 other people waiting for the starting gun.

Running the Bidwell—and I use the word running very loosely—is for me a self-imposed trial by ordeal. There are real athletes running in this race. These are men and women with the fluid grace of felines, who practically dash the two laps around lower Bidwell Park that make up the course.

These people legitimately dream of winning the race, and of hearing the crowd at the finish line cheer as they break the tape. My goals are a bit more modest. I don't want to die. Beyond that, I want to finish. If in my wildest dreams I so much as fantasized about coming in first, I would be forced to publicly and humbly apologize to every other runner on the course.

After last year, I have added another goal to my Bidwell list. Success can be an enemy, and in 2005 I experienced a moment of personal achievement. I broke the three-hour barrier! Okay, it's not the four-minute mile or an eight-foot high jump, but for me it was astounding.

In past episodes of self-administered torture, during all the previous times I have spent slapping my sore, blistered feet on the pavement for 13 miles, it had taken me substantially more than three hours to finish. Officially, all runners are supposed to be off the course in 180 minutes, but the race organizers had pity on the strange old guy straggling in dead last, and they hung around until I finished.

Last year, when I finished in under three hours, I was so thrilled you'd have thought I had just earned a gold medal at the Olympics. Prior to this, finishing was enough. I had, under my own power covered 13 miles—13 freaking miles! That is a very long way and it is a hard thing to accomplish. I could take substantial pride in just doing this hard thing, but then I did a foolish thing. I got healthy enough to run just a little faster and—poof—I raised my expectations. Nothing is heavier than a raised expectation.

Last Saturday, finishing wasn't adequate. Not dying wasn't enough. This time I had an athletic feat to perform. Anything less than a sub-three hour race was going to be a failure. To add to my growing sense of panic, I found myself in the highly unlikely position of being another runner's "inspiration." Minutes before the race began, a perfectly charming woman arrayed in running togs trotted up to me. She recognized me from my picture on this column, a situation I dearly hate because I refuse to believe that ugly man in the photo looks like me.

She said when she read about me running in the Bidwell last year, it inspired her to try. So this year she turned 50 and she—by gosh—was going to follow my noble example. After the starting gun sounded she disappeared up ahead of me, but I got a report later.

My dear bride, the saintly Susan, who loves me even when I do really crazy things, was waiting for me at the finish line with a big hug, a bottle of water, oranges and a couple of homemade oatmeal-butterscotch cookies. As I gasped for breath, Susan said a nice woman had finished about 20 minutes in front of me. The woman said she had met me before the race and told me about being her inspiration. Then she added, "I haven't seen him lately, though. I hope he is okay."

For the record, I am okay. I lived. I finished, and I came in at 2 hours and 55 minutes. Even slow success can be sweet. Next year, who knows? Maybe 2 hours and 54 minutes is possible.

● ● ● ●

Taking a slow boat to nowhere

As diet and exercise have diminished the greatness of my person, my dear bride, the saintly Susan, and I have begun to explore activities that are more physically challenging than watching videos on the television. Doing healthy things—at least if not taken to irrational extremes—can actually be fun. Susan and I have gone on long walks, hiked into the foothills, and made tentative plans for even more ambitious outdoor endeavors.

For a long time Susan has discussed the possibility of we two taking to the local rivers and lakes in some flavor of human-powered water craft. She wanted to think about the two of us climbing into a canoe and paddling our way into the sunset. I have tried to arrange such an excursion a couple of times, but both opportunities evaporated when the canoe I had hoped to rent wasn't available on the weekend I had planned to use it.

Then a few weeks back Susan and I were wandering through one of those it-sells-everything-but-nuclear-weapons super stores, when I came across a potential option to the never available canoe. For a price that seemed reasonable, the store was selling a three-person, inflatable vinyl boat. This mini-boat was small enough that un-inflated we could toss it into the trunk of Susan's car, and it came with two paddles and an air pump to inflate the beast.

With our first-ever family reunion on the horizon, we decided our grandwidgets would get a kick out of the boat when we went on an already-scheduled trip to the lake. So we bought it. The grandkids did enjoy it, but Susan and I didn't get a real chance to check it out.

A few weeks later, when we planned an extended weekend escape to Lake Tahoe, we packed the boat along with our luggage.

It is worth mentioning at this point there is a significant difference between paddling a canoe through placid lake waters, and trying to propel a semi-circular inflated raft over the same space. However, without benefit of any experience in that regard nor evidence of even marginally good sense on my part, we launched our little craft into the water.

The paddles were mounted rowboat-style on either side of the craft, which meant the most effective means of propulsion was rowing backwards. While rowing backwards gets you there faster, it also means you tend to see where you've been rather than where you are going.

That point was underscored when I paddled us right into the side of an anchored and occupied cabin cruiser, while the astonished owner and his family watched. I explained I was sorry and had no idea what I was doing—which was itself more or less obvious—as I tried to maneuver our boat out of his way.

It was about this point that Susan, fearful that I would row us into the path of an oncoming speedboat, suggested—read that demanded—that we find a way to share the paddling duties. She took over one paddle, while I took the other, and we made a serious effort to coordinate our strokes to make us go in one planned direction. Surprisingly we actually reached a point where we could make this unlikely arrangement work. We had stroked along for about half a mile or so when Susan and I got out of sync.

The boat that had been moving more or less effectively suddenly began to spin in place. It was about that time that an El Dorado County sheriff's patrol boat came into view. I'm sure the deputies saw our little craft spinning and came to the not unreasonable conclusion that we had no clue what we were doing.

As the cop boat turned in our direction, we sort of regained control of the Good Ship Lollipop and began creeping along the shore. The deputies apparently decided we were harmless and sailed on.

When we got within a couple of hundred yards of our destination, I rowed the boat close enough to the shore to allow me to jump out, and wading, I towed Susan and the vessel the rest of the way.

I learned a couple of important truths from that experience. First, the next such endeavor will involve a real canoe, and secondly, failure to apply sunscreen to one's legs can result in a truly impressive burn. I'm still peeling like a bright red banana!

● ● ● ●

Beauty is in the Eye of the Beholder—or is it?

I'm willing to concede beauty is in the eye of the beholder—heck, I always liked the looks of the Edsel and never understood what anybody saw in Brooke Shields—but I always thought ugly was a generally accepted absolute.

Ugly was something I could depend on. Unaltered by time or passing fad, ugly was an observable Rock of Gibraltar. But lately—in a world where an anorexic Ally McBeal can be a sex symbol and "grunge" clothing a fashion statement—I have been forced to consider the possibility that ugly is as much a matter of personal perception as beauty. This, in a round-about way, brings me to my shoes.

As part of my continuing, if spotty, effort to fight the battle of the bulge, I have been trying to walk and/or run on a fairly regular basis. By my definition "run" is any activity that moves me faster than a leisurely stroll.

This burst of allegedly healthy activity was just too much for my beloved tennies, which rapidly surrendered under the unexpected onslaught of my massive form pounding them relentlessly against the unforgiving pavement. The untimely death (I mean they were only seven years old!) of my tennies forced me into the unexplored wilderness of the sporting goods store.

The trip would have been truly frightening—after all slim, fit people hang out in such places—but I had the advantage of a trusted guide, my son, Matthew.

For the last few months, the Matt-man has been working in the store. He is the perfect retail salesman, handsome, personable, witty, and disgustingly sincere. This kid could sell cold drinks at the North Pole.

These attributes make him my candidate for the kid most likely to support his parents in a manner to which we would like to become accustomed when we become old and feeble, which in my case could be about next Thursday.

Matthew assured me if I dropped by the store he could fix me right up, and better still, he could get me a 15 percent discount.

In the past my shoe buying criteria have been simple: do they more or less fit, are they cheap, and are they black? To say I am conservative about my clothing is to have a great grasp of the obvious.

So my natural inclination was to head for a table piled high with marked-down, generally black shoes. With the practiced hand of a master, Matthew steered me to a wall where the shoes were gaudy in color and had prices that ran higher than my body temperature.

Before I could protest, or faint, Matt vanished into a back room and came out with a pair of shoes that looked like they had been caught in a paint store explosion. Green, gray, brown, navy blue, royal blue, yellow laces, I'm not really quick about such things but I knew for sure these shoes weren't black. I also knew they were genuinely ugly. Before I could protest, Matthew had stripped off my old shoes, slipped on these monsters and was lacing them up.

I had to admit they felt good, but when I said they were ugly, Matthew gave me the look he usually reserves for small children, very pretty girls, and the simple minded.

"Dad, those shoes are great. They're stylin'!"

Well, I have never in my life been stylin' before and the next thing I knew I was writing a check for twice what I had expected to pay, even with the 15 percent discount, and Matthew was guiding me to the door.

Now I own a pair of really comfortable, ugly shoes, but maybe they aren't so ugly. Perhaps I'm just . . . well . . . out of step. Maybe Brooke Shields is even good looking.

● ● ● ●

Grinding your way to health . . . and fatness

Like every other person in the known world, I want to make this body I drag around healthier. Unfortunately, my mortal form is in greater need of work than most people's. However, I've discovered a workout tool that is going to give me arms and shoulders that would make Arnold Schwarzenegger green with envy.

So when you see me on the street—three or four months down the road—and, while admiring my buffed physique, you ask, "What's your secret?" I'll whisper the two magic words.

"Wheat grinder."

I'm not talking about some sort of health food, or a magical power-drink that will alter my body and make my voice deeper through biochemical machinations. My wheat grinder is a manually operated device designed to turn whole grain wheat into flour.

We've had this beast hanging around the household for decades and for most of that time it lived—dusty and ignored—in the barn that was part of Casa Aylworth I. I sort of rediscovered it when my dear bride, the saintly Susan, and I moved into our current, much more sophisticated digs. I suppose I should admit I more or less forgot this hand-cranked relic of a different century existed.

Even when I moved it the first couple of times, I didn't think of it as much more than a rather ugly paperweight. However, in an effort to reach back to my pioneer roots, I was curious to see if the old mill still had the capacity to crunch wheat kernels.

I started out by methodically taking it apart, removing the ancient flour residue left in the works from some long-forgotten grinder, sanding away layers of rust, and oiling things that looked like they needed oil. When the maintenance was completed—strangely, it was a lot harder to put the mill back together than to take it apart—I threw a handful of wheat in the hopper and tried to turn the handle.

It was then I discovered that cranking a wheat grinder requires substantial effort and not just with the arm doing the turning. Despite the fact it weighs more than a Volkswagen Beetle, the whole mill wants to flip over with each crank. So, while one arm struggles to turn the crank the other is required to keep the grinder from tossing itself—and me—on the floor.

In the process of turning two cups of whole wheat into three cups of rather coarse flour, both my arms and shoulders informed me in no uncertain terms that this was in fact exercise. The level of self-inflicted pain was high enough to convince me I was doing my body the sort of worthwhile harm necessary to build muscle and—voila—a potential exercise craze, right up there with spinning, yoga and Pilates, is born.

All it really needs is a snappy catch-line. How about "grind your way to fitness," "achieving the flour of health," or maybe "bump and grind to a bodacious bod." OK, the slogans need some work, but the potential is there.

This might turn into a real money-maker. Heck, somebody made a ton of money on pet rocks. Compared to that, this is rocket science.

To make this work, all I need is enough wheat grinders to start a fitness class. Then I have to keep the idea quiet so nobody else can get on the grinder bandwagon before I can launch my million-dollar enterprise.

As a secondary benefit, I can start a bakery with all the flour the class will produce, which in turn will fatten up more people, who will need to get on the grinder to get back into shape.

In addition to being the next Mr. Universe, I do believe I'm a genius.

● ● ● ●

Some People Aren't Good at Being Sick

Recently I had the doubtful pleasure of being genuinely, sincerely and disgustingly sick, and, I've got to tell you, I don't do sick well.

I'm convinced that "good" sick people manage to suffer in noble silence. They bear their pestilential burden with stoic strength, treating even the most ghastly malady with cavalier indifference. For the record, I am not one of those people.

Thankfully, I don't get sick all that often, so I don't have much experience in the etiquette of the infirm.

This time I came down with a simple, garden variety cold, but the term *cold* is just such a weak and insipid word for the really impressive level of physical discomfort I was experiencing. In point of fact, I was sicker than two dogs and a pony named Fred!

Unfortunately this wasn't one of those illnesses that could offer the happy escape of imminent death. No, I was convinced I would live through this ordeal. I just didn't want to.

I'm not sure if it was from my great dedication to the journalistic profession or from a perverse desire to share this malady with my co-workers, but either way I dragged myself into the office a couple of times during the siege. I never made it much beyond half a day at the office, which was probably a good thing from my co-workers' point of view.

To make matters worse, I timed my plague horribly. A reasonably intelligent sick person would schedule his bout with disease at some point when his loved ones are near at hand to cater to his every need. I managed to come down with the cranky awfuls during a period when my dear bride, the saintly Susan, was either working at her office or, worse still, over a weekend when she was out of town.

Not only did I feel like the bottom of a birdcage, I didn't even have my lady love around to pat me on the head, and say, "Poor sweet baby!"

At a time when I wanted to bemoan the injustice of disease, and be pampered during my ordeal, I was home with two cats and a dog, who I have to say are really worthless at providing sympathy and medical care. Actually, our dog, Pirate, is good at the sympathy; it's the care you don't get.

I did manage to get out long enough to buy myself a quantity of orange juice. For reasons I have never fully understood, conventional wisdom holds one should drink lots of juice when one is sick. As far as I can tell, this makes no medical sense, but who am I to fight conventional wisdom? So I consumed gallons of juice, which meant I spent a significant part of my convalescence in the bathroom.

When I was a kid my mother convinced me that used liberally and in combination, layers of Vicks VapoRub and hot lemonade can cure all human disease. So I slathered myself in a reeking layer of stinky goo and brewed up a pot full of near boiling lemonade. The net result of that effort was I was so pungent that the four-legs in the household went from casual indifference to my suffering to outright rejection of my person.

In response to this abandonment by the critters I lovingly feed and shelter, I dipped myself a brimming cup of the lemonade and gulped it down. The net result of all this self-imposed therapy was I smelled so bad my critters couldn't stand me and I had a wonderful blister on the roof of my mouth, because hot is different from nearly boiling.

Well, to both my short-term chagrin and my long-term joy I have recovered from my viral onslaught. And after a series of showers to eliminate the Vicks odor, and some ice cream to help my mood and my blistered mouth, I am more or less back to what passes for normal.

However, I am committed to taking overall better care of myself. Being sick just isn't all that much fun, especially with the danger that I might live through it.

● ● ● ●

Being healthy apparently no excuse to avoid doctor

Monday I'm going to do something I really don't want to do. I'm going to see the doctor. No, I'm not sick and that's part of what makes an already disagreeable situation even more distressing.

It's not that I don't like my doctor. In point of fact, my physician is a prince of a fellow. Always smiling, he is extraordinarily patient with me as a patient. He is always willing to answer my endless questions when I do venture into his office, and never uses dull needles on me, even though I publicly admit to trying to avoid him. I avoid visiting my doctor professionally for the same reason I don't want to have professional contact with funeral directors, and I know a collection of really nice guys in both professions.

I want to visit a doctor when I have specific need for his or her services, and right now I feel truly dandy. That position makes perfect sense to me, but it is an argument that is totally lost on my dear bride, the saintly Susan. Lately my son, Adam, has also been challenging my logic.

Okay, I admit the obvious. I am in fact three days older than dirt, and I am . . . ah . . . er . . . well, shall we say "big boned?" All right, the reality is I am fat, but I am a disgustingly healthy fat guy. I work out multiple times a week. I run—well, more fairly, stagger—a half-marathon once a year. I don't smoke, drink or chase wild women— except for the one I married.

None of that seems to impress Susan or Adam. Recently, these people, who I am convinced love me, have been beating me up pretty good on this issue.

Adam works for an insurance company, and he is the best kind of a policy peddler. He not only cares about commissions, he cares about his clients. Lately some of those clients, or rather their heirs, have been cashing in on policies.

What bothers Adam most is: A) some of those clients have been materially younger than his dear old dad; and B) some of them have left this mortal sphere because of ailments that could have been easily treated had they been caught early.

I have long maintained that I am in fact immortal. As my hair has become more uniformly silver—that sounds so much better than gray—and the belt length has expanded, I've been forced to consider the possibility that I might have a date with the Grim Reaper at some time far in the distant future.

This past week Adam, his beautiful and enormously pregnant wife, Dana, and two of their three resident widgets gathered with Susan and me at a local restaurant for a family dinner. With Adam sitting on one side and Susan on the other, these two wonderful people did everything but batter me with a chair to get me to see a doctor. Adam gave me a running commentary on everybody he knows who has died any time in the last 22 years. He also told me in perfect detail how my insurance policy will happily pay me for certain forms of preventive maintenance.

Susan observed that we just got a nice check because she had a mammogram. Adam immediately said the company would pay me for a mammogram, too. After I gave him a you-have-well-and-truly-lost-your-mind look, he said, "We've all got the same tissues." Beyond that, according to my son, there is a whole list of other medical tests that would win me remuneration.

The problem with that is some of these tests involve inserting cameras into orifices where no camera should ever go.

However, I have surrendered to the inevitable. Tomorrow I'm surrendering my body to the poking, prodding, and—worse still—the probing associated with a full, thorough physical exam. While I look forward to the event with precisely the level of joy that I would a colonoscopy, I'm going to do it.

I have no reason, knocking loudly on the nearest wood, to believe my buddy the doctor will find anything that needs attention. But I'm going to the doctor because people who love me want me to and because I know for certain that Susan and Adam will kill me if I die of something that could have been fixed.

● ● ● ●

House Tales

I hate being a bachelor

My dear bride, the saintly Susan, has left me and I have to say I absolutely hate—read that loathe and despise—being single! I'm not talking *left*, as in "I've had it with you! Eat dirt and DIE!"

I mean Susan has *left*, as in packed her bags for a week working in Florida. After her week on the right coast, she is going to fly home just long enough to collect our globetrotting daughter, the darling Rebecca, and the two of them will drive off two states east. Becca is returning to college and her mom wanted to drive her out there.

Just to add a touch of frosting to this whole unhappy cake, Susan has a family reunion after that. The net result is for just about a month, I am playing the role of aged bachelor and I am something less than thrilled.

The fact of the matter is I don't have a great deal of practical experience when it comes to be a solo householder. I was in my first week of my freshmen year in college when I met the dark-eyed beauty with the crooked smile who would become the center and circumference of my world. Just a touch under two years later we were married, and since then the word "single" has had no place in my vocabulary.

Now I rattle around Casa Aylworth, which is devoid of children as well as spouse, like a monk in a seriously low rent monastery. However, my monastic existence does not include a vow of silence. I talk all the time, but now the hearers are all of the short four-legged variety.

I've always been inclined to talk to my two resident dogs, Che and Pirate, as well as the two cats, Koi and Kola, who think they own the place and are just a bit put out that I live there. However, while I usually talk to the animals, this lack of human contact at home has me waiting to see what the critters have to say in return.

So far none of the four have said anything that didn't sound like "meow" or "woof," which I suppose is a good thing. I mean if I start having full-on conversations with the household beasties, the debate over my alleged sanity will be decided conclusively.

But I do confess to getting a bit lonely.

I've reached the point where I hope some telemarketer will call at dinner time so I have someone to talk to. "No thank you. I really don't want vinyl siding, car insurance, an all-expenses-paid free vacation to Lodi that will only cost $1,200. Nor do I want to donate to the International Society to Put Diapers on Tree Crotches, but aside from that, telemarketer-person, how was your day today?"

I may be the only person in the history of the world to be hung up on by a phone solicitor.

All of this does tend to remind me how very much I appreciate my Susan, not that I needed a whole lot of reminding.

I suspect when my bride does come home she will guess by the way that I drop to the floor and start hugging her ankles that I missed her. The dogs and cats will probably be glad she is home too, because I'm sure they are tired of talking to me.

● ● ● ●

When mom leaves town

My beloved, the saintly Susan, is out of town for the weekend and the strangeness is about to begin. Since my widgets were old enough to take official notice they have always maintained that the household WQ (weirdness quotient) skyrockets when mom leaves.

Susan is the foundation of this collection of random wanderers. In a household where confusion is the norm, Susan is the calming voice of reason. She makes most of the meals, does most of the shopping, keeps all of the financial records, is the loving confidant, the motherly adviser, has maintained schedules for up to seven children and a mental midget husband, and accomplishes all these minor miracles while juggling her responsibilities as a university instructor, a novelist (she has six books in print and another coming out in December), and running a collection of other businesses.

I have trouble keeping two thoughts in my fading mind at any one time, and doing two things at once (walking and chewing gum, for example) is simply out of the question. So when one of her various hats draws Susan out of town things . . . ah . . . er . . . well . . . fall apart.

Without a doubt the first thing that collapses is the kitchen. One of the things that impressed me from the moment I met Susan was her almost magical ability to walk into a kitchen that appeared utterly empty to me, and come out with a meal that was not only fit for a king, but was sincerely healthy. To say I don't have my beloved's culinary talent is to have a firm grasp of the obvious. I have long recognized that cooking is not my strong suit.

When I was a Boy Scout, back in the Dark Ages, and I either ate my own cooking or starved, my lack of skill was cured with strawberry jelly. I learned no matter how badly I burned it, how oddly I spiced it, how utterly I translated good ingredients into gastronomic disaster, I could eat just about anything with enough strawberry jam on it.

I ate tin-foil dinners slathered in strawberry jam. I ate canned stew covered in strawberry jam, and even pork and beans with strawberry jam.

After years of often disgusting trial and error, I've found if I can cook it on a barbecue grill or fry it, there is at least a small chance I can produce something vaguely edible. But the kids like to keep a stash of ramen noodles around for when mom leaves.

Entertainment also changes. While I still ban televised wrestling from the household tube, we are likely to see videotaped movies that would have mom screaming and running in circles. Adventure films that have no noticeable plot, are utterly devoid of character development and primarily focus on some near-superman wielding an array of unlikely weapons, become the amusements of choice.

Dishes are only cleaned when mom is sure to be on her way home. Personal hygiene becomes spotty at best and testosterone flows like root beer. Rebecca, 15, who loves her dad and brothers, has learned to adjust to the male half of the family going slightly nuts. When she can, she schedules overnights so she is away from ground zero when mom is gone.

But then, like spring returning after winter, Susan comes back and brings sanity in her wake. Meals become edible again. Rebecca comes home, and somebody finally waters the houseplants.

● ● ● ●

Electrical woes: A curse to share

I have long admitted that I should not be allowed to use hand-tools, touch sharp objects, or have anything to do with electricity more technical than turning on a light, but I recently discovered that in at least one of these areas, I have shared my talents with my sons.

Not too long ago our trusty, and much abused, dishwasher gave up the mechanical ghost. My dear bride, the saintly Susan, took the position that with only four full-time residents in Casa Aylworth, we could hand wash the dishes for now. For the most part I bow to Susan's wisdom in all things, if for no other reason than she is materially smarter than I am, but when it comes to dishwashing I had to speak up.

When we were first married, Susan and I agreed on a division of labor. Susan hates to iron men's shirts, and I am no great fan of dish-washing, so I agreed to take care of my shirts, and my bride took over the sink duties. In the long run this has meant that the dishes almost always sparkle, and I wear a lot of wrinkled shirts. However, while I don't much like doing dishes, I really hate the feeling I am dumping on Susan, so with some difficulty I persuaded her of the propriety of replacing the now defunct dishwasher.

Buying a dishwasher was fairly easy, but when I got it home, it became painfully evident that the machine was not willing to install itself. That reality meant I might have to take the fearful step of picking up a tool.

That's when Paul stepped in.

Paul has spent all of his 21 years watching dad well and truly screw things up in the name of ineffectual home improvements. He reasoned, why let dad ruin things when he could easily take over and do things right? With that in mind Paul bundled Mom and Dad out of the front door with the promise, if we would get out of his way, he would happily install the machine all by himself.

We did as we were told and had a lovely Saturday afternoon. When we got home, we had a perfectly installed new dishwasher, but also had a story of the curse of the Aylworths.

It seems Paul assumed the breaker switch that turned off the lights in the kitchen also turned off the power to the dishwasher. He learned the error of his ways when an unanticipated burst of electricity left him quivering on the kitchen floor. Something, perhaps the sound of a minor lightning bolt or the smell of sizzling bacon, alerted Paul's older brother, John, that something was amiss.

When John found his brother on the floor, and determined he was still breathing and all of his usual parts and pieces seemed to be intact, he asked Paul, "Are your fillings hot?" No, I don't know what that was about.

I was telling Adam, my resident sons' older, married brother, of Paul's tale of electrical woe when I discovered electricity isn't Adam's friend, either. Adam told me that once, while living in Australia, he was trying to heat a pot of water on his electric stove. Wearing nothing more than a towel, and standing barefoot in a puddle of water, Adam decided to see if the water was hot by dipping a finger in the pot.

Apparently the combination of the puddle on the floor, bare feet, and the electrical heating coil under the metal pot, sent a not inconsequential burst of electricity through Adam.

The situation seemed so unlikely to Adam, that after shaking off the first shock, he promptly dunked his finger back in the pot to test if it had really happened. It had. When he stopped tingling for the second time, Adam—who has a reasonably twisted sense of humor—saw his roommate wander by, also barefooted.

Casually strolling out of the kitchen Adam yelled, "Hey, would you test the temperature of the water on the stove?" and then he waited, giggling, just out of sight.

Some curses are more fun than others.

● ● ● ●

Dealing with a bewitched clothes closet

I've discovered that my closet is magical, or maybe bewitched. Either way, it doesn't follow the normal rules of physics.

From my own widgethood I have recognized there is something inherently mystical about a closet. Back in the days when I was pretty sure girls were just boys with long hair who dressed funny, and a hard day at work meant I had to do my times tables clear up to 5s, I knew for an absolute fact my closet was haunted.

While I had never seen them, heard them, or been touched by them, I knew with a 9-year-old's absolute faith in the unreal that ghosts lurked in my closet, and that knowledge presented me with one of my first serious dilemmas.

Do I leave the closet door open or closed at night?

Since I could neither see nor hear my resident specters, I could never be sure if they were in the closet or out. If they were inside when I closed the door, that was good because they couldn't come out and "get me" while I slept. But if I closed the door, and I inadvertently locked the ghosts out of their closet abode, then the spooks would obviously get really mad, and then who knew what horrors might happen?

Since no phantom assaults ever disturbed my youthful slumber, I have to assume I always guessed right on the open/closed question. However, the sense that closets are mystical places never quite went away.

The other day I awakened with a disturbingly powerful urge to do something useful, and my closet was my chosen victim. Over the last few weeks my dear bride, the saintly Susan, has been quietly campaigning to upgrade my wardrobe. She has presented me with several pairs of pants and a whole batch of new shirts. Susan and I share a closet, and the flood of new duds filled my half of the already crammed thing right up to the bursting level.

So when I jumped from bed with this unaccountable burst of positive energy, I decided to get rid of clothing that was old, out of date, torn, didn't fit, or was just too ugly to be allowed out in public. Using that as a rigid standard, I figured by the time I finished going through my clothing, I would have enough space in the closet to park a Greyhound bus, if I had a bus.

I told myself to be ruthless. If I didn't love the article of clothing it was going to be history. I was going to go through my closet like Sherman on his way to the sea.

The only exception to this scorched earth policy was a couple of print shirts Susan gave me, including one with images of tigers and bamboo plants on it. Susan loves to see me in it, and even though I am convinced the Chinese characters printed on the garment translate to, "Look at this dumb shirt," good sense demands I wear what my wife likes. In an hour's time I had filled two big garbage bags with shirts and pants, but there was one problem.

The closet was still full!

Okay, math has never been my really strong suit, but I am pretty well convinced, if you take a number of things from a pile of things, at the end of the day, you should have fewer things in the pile, but apparently the closet doesn't believe in subtraction.

I confess, I'm not the least bit sure how to react to the cornucopia of shirts and pants. Given a choice I think I would prefer a never empty wallet, but that would be magic, and no sane person believes in magic.

● ● ● ●

Bigger may not always be better

I'm more than willing to admit it was stupid , but my heart—if not my lungs—was in the right place. From time to time I will go into an unexplained cleaning frenzy. The object of the assault need not be particularly dirty, but something snaps in my fevered brain and suddenly I am waving brushes and slathering cleaning products over the landscape.

While my dear bride, the saintly Susan, doesn't understand this behavior any more than I do, she generally approves; after all it keeps me busy and off the street. Where there is problem, it comes from my decidedly male approach to a project. I have this basic conviction that bigger is better.

If two aspirins are good, six must be better.

If a cute little campfire is cozy, a 20-foot-high bonfire is clearly superior.

If the recipe calls for one tablespoon of chili pepper, any fool can see it would be better with half a cup.

As a result my kids cringe when they know I'm cooking, and nobody ever lets me near the fire. All of that brings me to the ammonia.

My most recent attack of cleaning mania found me burrowing into a corner of my kitchen counter that is usually out of sight. When I moved enough small appliances, I found some genuine dirt. Inspired by the find, I grabbed the nearest form of cleanser, a quart bottle of ammonia, and sloshed a half-inch deep puddle over the counter.

Had I taken the time to read the bottle, I might have found out you are supposed to use this stuff in dilution, but knowing that bigger is better, I probably would have ignored the admonition, anyway.

At about this point Susan walked in and, watching me gasp for air, she immediately realized which stupid thing I had done this time. She tried to order me out of the kitchen, but between gasps I explained I was almost done.

In response, she explained why I was a total twit, which was pretty hard to debate at this point.

Her final admonition was, "You did this to yourself and I don't want to hear about your lungs hurting."

Well, of course not. I don't whine. I'm . . . ah . . . er . . . well . . . a man! That's true. It's also true my lungs feel like they have been sandblasted from the inside out, though I'll never admit that.

Nevertheless, I do think I might dilute the ammonia in the future.

●　●　●　●

Adjusting to pleasures and pains of new home

For better than two decades the clan Aylworth lived on sort of a mini-ranch that had the benefit of wide open space for kids to run, room for animals, and a plot for a substantial garden. With the exit of the last of the resident widgets, my dear bride, the saintly Susan, and

I have moved to a new house. This change of address has forced some substantial changes in our lifestyle.

For one thing we went from a lot size that allowed for horses, chickens and even an amazingly stupid flock of turkeys, to a chunk of ground that is only slightly larger than the house that is sitting on it. The reduction in acreage also meant I lost the garden space I had encouraged for a good many years. In point of fact the garden wasn't what you would call huge, about 40 by 30 feet, but the soil was gloriously fertile and after years of trying, it was closing to being rock-free.

Our new house is situated a few steps from another home being constructed by a dear friend and her husband. Besides building close by, the couple owns the empty lot immediately adjacent to our place. When I asked permission to garden their empty lot in exchange for a share of the produce, our friends readily agreed.

On the old property, when spring rolled around, I'd mow the over-winter weed-growth, rent or borrow a tiller, and make a couple of quick laps around the space. Then it was a matter of throwing down the seed and jumping out of the way.

While Casa Aylworth II is within sight of the ancient ancestral home, the soil type is remarkably different. The garden in the empty lot would make a great location for a gravel pit. I spent hours touring a materially smaller plot with a monster tiller, which proved to be an extraordinary rock finder. After hours of single combat with the would-be garden plot, I managed to gouge out a couple of inches deep of what amounted to coarse sand.

The tomatoes, peppers, garlic and squash I lovingly placed, and tended with infinite care—heck, I even spent time talking kindly to the wretched plants—functionally never grew at all. So much for the garden.

One of the things I never particularly appreciated about my previous home was the fact it was all electric. Aside from the fact the bills often looked like the national debt, we got our water from a well, by way of an electric pump. The water was great, cold, clear and pure, but when the lights went out, the water also stopped.

Not being able to get water from the tap is inconvenient, but that rapidly escalates to downright obnoxious when you realize that also puts the bathroom out of commission. The lack of a functional loo often forced us into some less aesthetically pleasing options. Horse stalls can be used for a multitude of things besides housing horses.

When we moved to the new house we got gas for heating, and municipal water. That meant that when the lights went out, as they did a couple of weeks back, wonder of wonders the taps and toilets were in full operation, but there was a "but . . ." to that.

When we designed the new house, we opted for on-demand water heating. There is a really neat little box in the garage that produces endless hot water, but only when somebody turns on a hot water tap. This was ecologically appropriate and I figured it would save a few nickels over the old tank method.

Well, I came home from the gym, drenched in sweat and smelling like a particularly stinky goat, to discover the electricity was off. No worries! All is well, well almost. The nifty gas-burning water heater has an electrical gizmo that is essential to its operation. No working gizmo, no hot water. Unfortunately I was way too disgusting to just wait until the power returned.

It was easily the coldest, and probably the briefest, shower I have ever had. Susan, always an insightful observer, said she could tell I'd had an interesting shower based on the high-pitched shrieks echoing down the stairs.

Even with the problems, I've come to appreciate the new house. If I can arrange to avoid getting too stinky while the power is off, everything should work out just super.

Long-awaited miracle about to become home

After much anticipation, a small and admittedly rather confusing family miracle is about to take place. Sometime in the next handful of days my dear bride, the saintly Susan, and I are going to move into Casa Aylworth III. The house we have been dreaming about, fretting over, and amazed by will become home.

For the last several months we have been visiting the house while it was under construction. We were thrilled when the land was graded, fairly bounced up and down for joy when the foundation was poured, and gazed in rapt wonder when the framing got underway.

Our friends rapidly recognized we (mainly me, actually) were a bit on the obsessed side when it came to the house.

Susan and I spent hours at the kitchen table in our old home, studying the floor plan for "the big house." We discussed furnishings, color schemes, and "window treatments." Prior to this experience I frankly thought a "window treatment" was some sort of a medical procedure. I also had no clue what a sconce was, until my beloved announced we would have two of them in the formal parlor.

We planned for the office, and where the big screen television would go (that was my part of the planning). Then the foundation was poured and the world made a turn.

Somehow, and I am by no means sure how, the house got reversed. The garage that was going to be on the right was on the left, and everything else was a mirror image of what we had been planning.

Tony, the incredible gentleman who is building the house, was chagrined by the reversal of foundation fortunes and actually offered to have the entire thing smashed up and redone, which seemed a little bit over the top even in my neurotic state. We began seeing the world in mirror image.

Every step since then has been a succession of tremendous "OOOOs! AHHHHs!"

The lighting fixtures went in. "OOOO!"

The walls were painted. "AHHH!"

When the counter tops were installed, I realized my new home has more exposed granite than any other place in California except Yosemite.

In days we will be moving into a house that is almost twice the size of the one where we raised our kids, with three bathrooms for two as opposed to the old days, when we had one bathroom for nine.

It is a little bit upside down, but it is not like we won't be populating the place with a set of rug rats. Besides our two cats and two dogs, we are planning on making this place Grandwidget Central.

We will have more attractions than Disneyland to entice our small—and not so small—descendants from all over the continent. We will have plenty of space for them and their parents, and we will revel in having them around.

There is also a garage with space for both Susan's car and MAH TRUCK. I'm not sure how my beloved pickup will react to having a place to rest out of the elements, but I suspect she will adjust.

The kitchen is big enough to feed the entire Mongolian Camel Corps, without having to eat in shifts.

Every room in the house, and the back porch as well, has ceiling fans, and I have a sneaking hunch, if we get all of the fans on high at the same moment, the house may lift off its foundations.

I also will have an official, built-in, no kidding workbench in the garage. Having a place to work on projects won't mean I'll be any better at them, but at least when I mash a finger with the hammer, I won't have to bleed on the dining room table any more.

The place is going to be a joy and it is going to be the house I share with the woman I love, which by definition makes it home to me.

Wife shows courage in leaving spouse home

I've always been a big fan of my dear bride, the saintly Susan, but I never knew how brave she was before she left for Bolivia.

I'm not talking about the courage it takes to head off into the high—as in 14,000 feet above sea level—Andes, or dealing with Bolivian white spiders, they aren't deadly but they are obnoxious; or living in a world where she has to build a fireplace in her living room.

For a woman who has mothered seven children—six of them boys—all of that is a stroll in the park.

No my sweet Susan demonstrated her extraordinary courage by leaving me to decorate our brand new home.

We had just moved into the new Casa Aylworth when Susan boarded the great silver bird and headed off to the land southward. While we had purchased some furniture, the walls were bare.

That meant she took off leaving me with better than two months of solo time to well and truly put my "mark" on our new domicile.

I'm sure she left knowing that was a real leap of faith.

About 10 years ago Susan went away for a weekend, and when she came back she found I—more or less with the help of the resident widgets—had taken our calm, sedate pale green bathroom and painted it wild, raging, screaming yellow,

This yellow was so bright and so high-gloss reflective that the little bit of sunlight that came through the narrow window in the shower made the entire room glow.

It was so intense that for the first several weeks after it was painted everybody in the family periodically stopped to turn off the light in the bathroom, which was never on.

So here I am with a blank canvas as far as the new house is concerned, functionally unlimited time, and no sane person around to keep me in check.

Given my druthers, I would tend to paint all adjoining walls in different, vivid colors.

I'd love to see the living room with one wall painted hot pink, with the adjacent walls concord grape purple, raging canary yellow, and vivid royal blue on the wall across the room.

I'd like to put fire engine red 70s shag carpet on the ceiling, and put lava lamps around the room as accents.

I've always liked mobiles—particularly things with silver dolphins—which I could spread sort of randomly around the house.

Out front I was thinking a nice big palm tree could be fun. Susan likes palm trees so she might even go for that.

I'm thinking about putting a Navajo rug up on the purple wall and on the pink wall I have this great print of Vincent van Gogh's "Starry Night."

Then in mid-June when Susan comes home, we can pass in review when I leave for Bolivia after she kicks me out for "ruining" her dream home.

OK maybe I'll stick to a few family pictures on the walls and nice—read that boring—beige paint.

Flights of fancy are a fun diversion, but in the final analysis, I'd rather have a happy spouse than a multi-hued house.

● ● ● ●

Moving proves to be more like a marathon

For the better part of three years I've been involved in a project that I thought was supposed to be an event, not a lifestyle. In April of 2005, I launched into an experience that I had avoided for the previous 22 years. I began moving from one home to another.

After rearing all seven of our widgets in the hovel I called Casa

Aylworth, my dear bride, the saintly Susan, and I were moving to a brand new—as in nobody had ever lived in it before—home. It was about the same square footage as Casa Aylworth I, so logic would suggest that everything that had been in the old house would fit into the new one, but logic has nothing to do with moving.

Casa Aylworth I was not much bigger than a walk-in closet, but came with a substantial barn and a pump house, both of which were crammed to the rafters with things that can only be called junk. However, junk that you have had for two decades becomes more important just by virtue of time of possession.

I filled two 20-yard trash bins with the worst of the worst. I also filled every possible space in Casa Aylworth II. When the new house was at capacity, I piled the remainder floor-to-ceiling into a 10-by-20 foot mini-storage locker.

Over the next 16 months two miraculous things took place: We moved again, from Casa Aylworth II into Casa Aylworth III, and the stuff in the storage locker, to which we did not add, somehow multiplied and expanded into another locker halfway across the town.

Casa Aylworth III is a mystical place. It is the only house I have ever been in with more storage space than I had stuff to store. The problem was when we resumed the ongoing joy of moving, some of the stuff that had been in Casa Aylworth II migrated to storage because it was old furniture that was just too breathtakingly ugly to move into our "dream house."

We've been in the dream house for 18 months, and a couple of months back Susan . . . ah . . . er . . . well . . . *suggested* that it might be a good time to get out of at least one of the storage lockers.

With that as motivation I ventured back into the musty mini-storage. I was immediately struck with a question: "Why the heck did I keep this crap?" I have a bunk-bed set that was way beyond worthless when I pulled it out of Casa Aylworth I, but there it is sitting in two different storage units. There are big boxes full of homemade videotapes. Remember videotape, the stuff you used way back before DVDs? These are mainly bad movies that I taped right off the television, commercials included. I never watched these tapes when I had a working VCR, which I no longer have. Even so, for reasons beyond the understanding of mere mortals, I carefully boxed these stupid tapes and packed them away in storage.

There were bales of fabric fragments that I somehow convinced myself Susan would want someday. I found a box full of university texts that one of my grown and gone widgets had probably never opened to begin with. Did I really believe somebody would want to read "Studies in Micro Economics," or "Introduction to Pre-Calculus?"

What sort of insanity possessed me when I carefully stored a cheap and broken fly rod, when (A) it doesn't have a reel, and (B) I don't fly fish?

As of now, we still have stuff and junk in both lockers on opposite sides of town. Susan has given away mountains of "quilt scraps." Some long-misplaced houschold treasures are back in their rightful places, displayed on shelves or in cupboards. And Casa Aylworth III still looks like we moved in yesterday. Boxes of something are piled in the spare bedrooms and there is no end in sight.

I foresee a far-distant future when the last box is empty and everything will be neatly stored in the house, put on display, or shipped off to a permanent home in the landfill. The problem is I have this terrible hunch that I will finally reach that point—two days before we decide to move to Casa Aylworth IV.

● ● ● ●

"Have you Got a Place for That?"

It began with a big smile, enough gold chains to give anybody a bad case of disco fever, and the same meaningless question, "Where you from?"

My dear bride, the saintly Susan, and I had done sort of a foolish thing, so naturally we decided to enjoy it. Some months ago a telephone solicitor called our home with this "super, stupendous, colossal deal of the century."

I know as a given any time I see something described in those terms—that is not the Ringling Brothers Barnum and Bailey Circus—I'm about to get my pocket picked. In this case the deal of the century involved a three-day vacation in San Francisco, with dinners, and theater tickets thrown in, all if Susan and I would sit through a pitch on timeshare vacations.

Since I have been on an extended diet, I've learned to say "no" to sweet confections I find a lot more attractive than over-priced vacation packages, so I figured saying "no," and "NO," and "NO!!!" repeatedly to some salesperson would be no challenge.

As a result we signed up for a room in a fancy downtown hotel.

I grew up in San Francisco, and while I have been back dozens of times since I called the city home, I've always previously been there as a tour guide. This time it was just Susan and me, and our entire goal was to be tourists on somebody else's bill.

Our hotel was literally across the street from Chinatown, and my dear bride and I planned to do some sincere window shopping. The shopping was made a touch more serious because we are going to be moving into a new home and for the first time in our married lives, Susan is actually getting the chance to "decorate" a house, as opposed to buying cheap and making do.

Besides visiting the places where a tourist in a loud Hawaiian shirt can buy tin cable cars that play "I Left My Heart in San Francisco," Susan and I were going to stores that were a bit further up the retail food chain and sold furniture rather than trinkets.

Like the pair of bumpkins we appeared to be, we wandered into this store, and began looking seriously at couches, marble-topped tables, chandeliers, and carpets. We had no more than stepped over the threshold when, Benjamin—gold chains and all—bustled up to us.

Big smiles and "Where-ya from?" oozed out of him like cheap cologne. When he saw as linger by any piece more than 2.8 seconds, "Have you got a place for that?" he asked.

Prices for everything were astronomical. "Ah, but we have to move everything. Today—for this moment only—the price would be a third or a fourth of astronomical."

If we had a way to transport Benny's "treasures" home, we might have actually purchased something, but since we couldn't, we reluctantly left. Down the street a block there was another store with almost the same merchandise, and as we entered, Benny's clone, complete with smile, gold chains and "Where-ya from?" bounded up to meet us.

His prices were equally astronomical, "Ah but," they were about to go from a furniture to a diamond store and "today—for this moment—only" the price could be slashed, just for us.

OK, I was born on a Thursday, but it wasn't last Thursday, and these pitches were far too verbatim. Were the businesses connected? "Oh no! What an idea!" and incidentally, "Have you got a place for that?"

Before the day was over we found the same furniture, the same gold chains, and the same pitch, "We are changing from a furniture store to a jewelry store and all this has to go," at two more locations within walking distance.

I had never realized how much fertilizer was regularly spread over the streets of my old hometown, but I had never been there as a tourist before.

By the time Susan and I headed home that weekend we had said no to a variety of hucksters, who all clearly believed in the P.T. Barnum maxim, "There's a sucker born every minute."

At least for that minute I wasn't the one. It may yet turn out that some day I'll have a place for that, but not real soon.

● ● ● ●

Moving is Not an Event; It is a Lifestyle

If you say it out loud—"I just moved into my new house"—it sounds like moving is a finite event, but that simply isn't true. Shifting one's life, domestic critters and belongings from one domicile to another is not a thing that happens on one given Saturday and is over.

Over the last 18 months—after 23 years in the same place—my dear bride, the saintly Susan, and I have moved twice.

Susan, as an example of her exceptional wit, intelligence and good planning, took off for South America as Move One was getting underway. It seems that she managed to be among the missing for the first stages of Move Two as well, but I have a hunch her memory differs on that one.

Be that as it may, moving is not a thing. It is an on-going trial by ordeal. Like being sent up the river, this sentence is for an indeterminate period, but you don't get time off for good behavior.

There does come a day when the big things—the bed, the piano, the couch and the cat condo Susan made for our felines out of scrap lumber and carpet fragments—are all in place.

It gives the mover the false sense of accomplishment and the hopelessly optimistic impression the job is done, but then there are THE BOXES!

Our first adventure in moving took us from our home of 22

years, that included a large barn and therefore a big bunch of storage space, to a pleasant if small home with no barn.

By way of translation that meant we had a whole bunch of stuff without a place to put it. Enter the storage unit.

I rented one of those surrogate garages, which I promptly filled to the rafters with things that were clearly way too valuable to throw away. For most of a year these boxes of treasures sat, patiently waiting for my return. Now we have finished Phase One of the ongoing water torture that is Move Two, and the time has come to transplant my glorious collection of cherished keepsakes. The problem is, I can no longer find them.

Oh, I can find the storage locker and the boxes I put in the locker are still there, but for the life of me I can't imagine why I kept most of this crap.

I have boxes—many, many boxes—filled with bad movies that I videotaped off the television. These are videotapes that I never watched in all the years they crowded an ancient entertainment center, that migrated to the landfill itself a long time ago.

I kept a pair of desks that no self-respecting junk shop would allow on the premises.

There are things in there worth keeping, such as my mother's silver set, my dad's oak desk, but to reach those I have to claw through a pile of what can only be described as debris.

So now I face another extended filtering process, where I will try to separate the trash from the treasures one more time.

My success in the last round leaves me with little hope that I will do any better this time. Part of the problem, and I freely acknowledge this, is I am a dedicated pack rat. Once I get my hands on something—almost any something—I find myself saying, "Someday I'm going to need this again."

The fact that no person—living or dead—could possibly come up with a shred of rational proof that anybody would want this particular item again, has no bearing on my alleged thinking.

Having said that I suspect I will continue the tortuous process of moving—and occasionally throwing away something—for years yet to come. I also suspect that when the day comes that I find myself pushing up daisies, my widgets will be faced with the chore of sorting through what is left in the storage locker. Without much effort I can hear them asking, "Why did Dad keep this garbage?"

To which I would have to answer, "I don't have a clue."

* * * *

Animal Tails . . . , er, Tales

Stilling the Coyote Chorus

I'm willing to admit running around outside in my underwear is more than enough to outrage public decency and put even my flagging sanity in doubt, but it seemed like a good idea at the time.

It was just before 2 a.m. when our two resident mutts, Taz and Che, began to bark like Lassie trying to tell the family the barn is on fire.

I had watched Lassie in my youth, and I have a barn, so like it or not, I was forced from the comfort of my much-loved waterbed to investigate. It was then I heard the coyotes.

While I live about five minutes' walk—if you walk very slowly—from the questionable glories of the civilized world, I am more or less surrounded by empty fields, and coyotes are frequent visitors.

In the past these four-footed marauders have stopped by to take one or more of my chickens to lunch, and while the birds may feel honored by the invitation, I don't think they really enjoy being the central attraction at a coyote feast.

So when a coyote glee-club began a jam session just outside in the darkness, I darted out to save my little feathered friends. Just what I could have done—half-naked, barefooted and empty handed—to dissuade any dedicated coyote gourmet from turning one of my birds into cold cuts, I have no idea.

If the entire coyote drum and bugle corps had decided to parade through my front yard yodeling the Washington Post March, there wouldn't have been much I could have done about it—considering my situation at the time.

To make matters worse, the post-midnight temperature had tumbled to a level that would have given a polar bear goose bumps. For the most part, I don't get cold. I think it comes from the fact I have a physique not unlike that of a walrus.

The saintly Susan, who would choose to sleep under six blankets and a goose down comforter on the hottest night of the year, says if I had an Indian name it would be "Sleeps Naked in a Blizzard."

But this was different. This wasn't cold; it was cryogenic.

Even so I stood there, stalwart defender of poultry, freezing my not inconsequential fanny off, expecting at any minute that a giant, ravenous coyote would materialize out of the darkness, rip the bolted door off the coop and begin shredding chicken *al fresco*. The monster never came, and even the coyotes at the impromptu jam session apparently had enough sense to stop singing and seek shelter. Not me.

When my shivering reached a point where the last few function-ing brain cells in my head realized I was in greater danger of dying from exposure than my chickens were from the coyotes, I returned babbling to my bed.

"I think my brain is frozen," I told my barely conscious bride.

"You're just discovering that?" Susan murmured.

"Why did I go out there? Why did I stay out there? What did I think I was going to do? Why do they put worms in those bottles of Mexican liquor?" I asked her.

Even I don't know where the last question came from. Susan just groaned and gave me clear, if surprisingly colorful, suggestions about what to do with my mindless mutterings.

I'm just glad my handful of neighbors slept through my noctur-nal wanderings. If I had been caught half-naked, blue and mumbling mournfully about shredded chickens, I'd probably be packing a moving van about now.

Short of signing myself into the loony bin, leaving town would have been my only option.

●　●　●　●

I have a cat with an identity crisis

Spats is a gray tabby who started out life as a tom cat but has had his attitude surgically adjusted. We got him as a barely weaned kitten and he grew up with two dogs as company—and that may be the core of his problem.

Cats, almost by definition, are independent sorts, not pets but co-habitants who allow humans to share their space, as long as we humans don't get in the way. Cats don't like dogs or small children, and turn up their noses at table scraps, but not Spats. I wonder from time to time if Spats thinks he's a dog or a people. In any event, I'm not at all sure he thinks he's a cat.

Spats comes when he's called, eats dry food without complaint, and seems to enjoy it when the dogs lick his head. The dogs have taught him to eat table scraps and to grab drinks from the toilet. He used to make his toilet runs only when nobody was looking, but now he sits outside of the occupied bathroom and yowls to get in for a drink.

The creature has some vaguely feline instincts. For one thing he can and does catch mice, and that's becoming a problem.

Our home is in an essentially rural setting even though the city is closing in. With acres of open grasslands around us, we also have acres of field mice. Spats has developed a talent for capturing the little beasties. The problem is he doesn't catch the ones that have set up residence in my walls. Spats catches mice outside and then brings them home. I don't know if he thinks he's sharing food or just wants us to meet his new little friend, but he tends to capture the critters essentially uninjured and then deposits them in the middle of the living room.

The suddenly freed mouse beats a hasty retreat under the couch and immediately joins a growing domestic population. We humans run in circles and the cat sits happily on the couch watching the performance.

My saintly wife, Susan, was in the process of climbing into the shower one day when she found it was already occupied by a little gray rodent. Sharing showers with mice is not too high on her happy list, so donning a towel, she called in Spats. Spats probably figured she was offering him a toilet tank libation and it took her a few minutes to direct his attention away from the commode and to the shower.

As soon as Spats saw the mouse, he understood his duty. With speed and grace he captured the critter and burst out of the tub and through the bathroom door. Once in the living room, he released the mouse he had rescued from the porcelain jail and sent it off to run and play.

I would consider the situation hopeless but recently Tazzie, my McNab Hound—English pointer cross pooch, has begun catching and eating gophers in the garden. Maybe she can explain the facts of life to Spats.

● ● ● ●

The chicken came first

I've reached the point where I'm trying to give them to strangers. "Hi. My name is Roger. Can I give you some of my eggs?" I find the conversation tends to stop there as the stranger hurries down the street. But I've got no choice. I've got to do something.

Maybe I should start from the beginning. I can answer the great eternal question. The chicken came before the egg. Or, more precisely, 19 hens came first.

When I got the 24 baby chicks, I knew about half of them or more would be roosters. I also knew with six children living at home, five of them large sons, we could consume a prodigious number of eggs. When five of the baby birds fell victim to a dog that thought "chick" was the English translation of *hors d'oeuvre*, the problem of egg production was even less.

Two things happened to change everything. First, three of the six Aylworth widgets fled the household—two to marriage and the third left the continent. Then, against all odds, all 19 chickens grew to be robust hens. The birds proved early on they had a talent as watch chickens, attacking every human being who wanders into their line of sight. As the chickens aged, they have demonstrated a second talent. These hens can make eggs!

We are getting 19 eggs a day, and they aren't neat about it, either. Any box, crevice, bucket or chair in the barn can be the nest *du jour*. We have one chicken who seems to be . . . well . . . retarded. She may settle into a nest to pop out a double-yolker, but she is just as likely to drop an offspring on the lawn without seeming to notice at all.

The saintly Susan has responded to the deluge of eggs as best she can. Chili *rellenos*, once an occasional treat, have become a mealtime mainstay. We have proof, in terms of the two teen males who still live under my roof, that real men do eat quiche. Egg nog isn't just for Christmas anymore and custards are good, too. I haven't checked, but I expect the collective cholesterol level of my family would give a cardiologist a heart attack.

But it doesn't stop.

The refrigerator is filled with eggs. They are in cartons, boxes and bowls. Eggs that can't find space in the refrigerator fill boxes on the kitchen counters. Rebecca, who often is blessed with the opportunity to hunt eggs, takes a shopping bag on her missions.

The filled bags are likely to get as far as the dinner table and stop. I'm becoming increasingly concerned that some of these non-refrigerated eggs are likely to turn into toxic waste before I can get rid of them.

There was a period of time, around Easter, when I was able to empty the entire kitchen of eggs. But that only lasted a day or two.

Until next Easter, I'm going to gift wrap packages of my oldest eggs and leave them sitting on the back seat of my unlocked car when I park at the mall.

● ● ● ●

Beware of Chickens

I have two dogs, a collection of firearms, a pair of sons and a two-fisted daughter living at home, but when it comes to home security I depend on my chickens.

I have 18 hens and they may be the only flock of attack killer chickens on the planet. We raised these critters from day-old chicks and from the morning they arrived in a cardboard box. When they got old enough and large enough to crowd our coop, my saintly wife, Susan, began leaving the coop door open during the daylight to let the birds range.

Once out of the coop the birds contented themselves by ridding the yard of anything that might be chicken edible and fertilizing everywhere they went. It wasn't until they started ranging that we discovered we had a flock of guard chickens. The problem is these birds know people are the givers of all food, and no matter how often they are fed they still want more. By way of the chicken psyche it's fairly simple: *People give us food. So if you see a people chase it until it feeds you*—and chase they do.

Imagine you've just stepped out of your car. From every direction you hear the bushes rattle and suddenly there they are, killer guard chickens.

Gullumping from one short leg to another, 18 plump hens join in a wobble-butted gallop, and they are all coming at you! Black, red, white and multi-colored, they careen across the uneven grass. (It's not really grass, it's mowed weeds, but why admit that?)

The chief hen, an unpleasant black feathered creature, with a single bright yellow toe on the claw of her right foot, whom Susan has named Harriett, leads the flock in pecking your feet. What they can't peck they poop on.

All of this would be wonderful, in a sort of way-out-there way, if my killer guard chickens could tell the good guys from the bad guys. The hens assail me with the same gusto they would a burglar. They attack me, my kids, the saintly Susan, our dogs, the neighbor's dogs— anything that arrives on legs and doesn't have feathers.

They will drive away door-to-door salespeople with the same clucking joy they would assault the Publisher's Clearinghouse prize patrol. No one and nothing is entirely safe . . . well except for my 17-year-old son, John.

John has developed a special . . . ah . . . er . . . well . . . relationship with the chickens. He has turned the chicken's propensity to pursue people into something of an art form. From time to time, John will bound out the front door, like a berserk ballerina, shouting, "Come my children!"

When the flock gathers at his heels, he proceeds to skip and jump and bound across the front lawn. The hens, waddling in tight formation, scurry from one side of the yard to the other, trying to keep time to John's frantic tempo.

At least we aren't raising emus.

●　●　●　●

She came, she saw, she took him away

We raised him up from his birth until he reached the very picture of the beautiful male, and now he is gone. It is a hard thing to deal with. I will miss him. He was always so cheerful, and so vocal in the morning.

Then, when his girlfriends all vanished, the saintly Susan took the amazing step of placing a classified ad for him. I was a little shocked, but what was I to say? I suppose I should not have been particularly startled when the phone began ringing immediately.

Susan would answer the callers' questions. She extolled his beauty, his mild personality, and lamented his lack of female companionship. Then one of the callers wanted to arrange a meeting. When she arrived, I realized we were in trouble. Pretty, tanned, sunglasses, shorts, she wanted to meet him, and as soon as she saw him, she was sure.

"He's beautiful," she murmured.

It was clear this lovely lady was immediately smitten with him, his bearing, the way he walked, and his powerful male voice. She wanted him.

If you have a large family, and we do, you get practiced at saying good-bye. First our widgets, and then our grandwidgets, have said farewell to home and hearth, and headed out into the big world, but not like this. This was so mechanical, so much like commerce. No money changed hands, it was not that sort of a deal, but it did have a decidedly meat market aspect.

She was gentle, and she seemed kind. She told us how she had moved into her present home, just to make space for somebody like him, and he was everything she had hoped for. Even so, the pretty woman didn't ask to talk to him. She didn't want to know about his tastes, or what he did for fun. She wanted to take him home, to possess him. Functionally, she wanted him caged. She even told me how she wanted him contained. She wanted me to help, and reluctantly I agreed.

Initially, I'd planned to sneak up on him in his sleep, and catch him that way, but as the woman was driving away, he wandered by, and I just knew I had him. He didn't want to go. He ran from me. When finally I cornered him, he fought hard—and I have the marks to prove it.

He didn't understand that even though I'm older, I'm more crafty, and as much as he would deny it, I'm stronger. The outcome was a foregone conclusion, and in the end I pushed him into the cat-carrier she had left to hold him. He didn't fit all that well. A full-grown Rhode Island Red rooster is bigger than a cat, but it was the best his new owner had to offer.

When she returned, she cooed over the shiny red rooster with the billowing tail. He was going to a good home, she assured me. He would have lots of hens to keep him company. The woman and her husband had a big coop, and a fenced chicken yard. The rooster would be treated like a king.

I'm willing to admit he has gone on to a far better place. Certainly it was going to be a far better place than where his hens went. At one point the rooster led a flock of about two dozen hens, but over the years a combination of coyotes and later, neighbor dogs, paid a few visits, and took the girls out to lunch. The rooster could run a little faster and avoided the canine invitations.

Now, with no hens to keep him company, and with residential subdivisions popping up around the Casa Aylworth like so many toadstools, the rooster and his lusty pre-dawn crow had no future.

That's why Susan suggested—read that, I would be sharing the coop with the rooster if I ignored this suggestion—that the rooster needed a new home.

As the lady drove off with the rooster, I confess to a certain wistful moment. I may be the only person with in a three-mile radius who would say this, but I'm going to miss his crowing, and he really was pretty.

● ● ● ●

Confronting the demon in the barn

I've waded through icy floodwaters, chased after a tornado, raced to the scene of a deadly earthquake, had a crazy man point a loaded pistol at my sweet innocent face, and lived through having seven teenage children get drivers' licenses. All of this is to point out that—except for spiders of any size and the IRS—there aren't too many things that really scare me. I have now added the "devil kitty" to my list of personal terrors.

As horror stories always do, this started on a dark cold night. It was a Wednesday, to be precise. On Wednesdays I have a routine. Thursday mornings are trash pickup in my neighborhood, so, if I want to get my garbage collected, I have to drag the can to the curb Wednesday night.

At Casa Aylworth, the curb is nearly 200 yards down a gravel driveway from my front door, and when I drag the can down to the road I bring my barrel-bodied black Lab Che with me. Che was hit by a car last year and the poor old girl has a little trouble getting around. I've found if I take her on walks it helps keep my old furry friend from just congealing. One of those walks is the scheduled Wednesday night trash stroll.

We were making our return trip. Che had happily gamboled down the driveway with me. I heard it just as we passed the barn. Out of the darkness came the most unearthly, guttural, gravel-voiced wail. With the hair standing up on the back of my neck, I turned at stared at the noise.

The sound seemed to be coming from the barn, and I have to admit I wouldn't have been all that shocked to catch the smell of brimstone on the breeze, or see a red glow coming from the windows, where the portal into hell itself had clearly just opened.

Every time a doorway to Hades appears in my front yard, I respond by running into the house, which I did. Che, despite her disability, beat me into the house, and had the commendable good sense to go hide in a back bedroom.

I suspect I sounded just as entirely freaked as I felt, when I yelled to my son, Paul, to back me up as I confronted a demon in the barn.

Paul is 21 and he has seen his daddy go off the deep end more than once. I rather suspect he thought I had just lost it one more time, but because he loves me—and tends to take pity on the feeble-minded—he followed me into the darkness.

You don't go off to face down an emissary from the hot regions bare handed. So I took a flashlight and trusty .22, and Paul carried a machete, as we ventured forth.

I babbled to my son about the horrible, evil sound coming from the area of the barn, but the screeching had stopped by the time we left the house, which further convinced Paul that I had lost the last two of my remaining brain cells.

Then he heard it. Somewhere between the sound of an infant with a bass voice screaming its lungs out, and an cry of animal being fed backwards into a meat grinder, the noise assaulted our ears.

We crept up on the barn with sure expectation that at any moment something out of a very bad nightmare would erupt right out of the ground and try to eat our souls.

The sound kept coming and we followed into the barn, to a vacant horse stall.

Peaking over the stall door I saw it . . . a big, black-furred, long-haired . . . kitty-cat.

The beast was noisy, and may have been the "devil kitty," but face-to-face it was roughly as frightening as five pounds of Cream 'O Wheat.

I have no clue why it was making the sound it was, because as soon as it saw me the critter dashed out of the barn, into the darkness.

I haven't seen—or heard—devil kitty since then, but I've taken to wearing a garlic necklace anytime I approach the barn after dark, just in case.

● ● ● ●

Critters teach lessons on clear communication

As a husband for 35 years and a father of seven widgets, I've stumbled across the not entirely shocking fact that communication is a truly wonderful thing. Perhaps surprisingly, I've found the four-legs that live in my house teach me a lot about clear, effective, and some-times messy communication.

Shortly after my dear bride, the saintly Susan, changed her last name to Aylworth, we adopted a tiny, half-starved, flea-ridden, tabby kitten which we named Packy. As cats will do, Packy almost immedi-ately declared herself the head of household and was gracious enough to allow Susan and me to share her space.

At the time I was too young, and way too unlearned in things feline, to understand that I was not only no longer king of the castle, but I didn't even have a vote.

I remember one morning getting dressed for work, and without thinking too much about it, I bounced my kitten off the bed. Packy was a whole lot more than unimpressed with my violation of kitty/human protocol, and she wanted to make sure I never made that mistake again. The palm-sized cat scrambled back up onto the bed, strutted up to where I was sitting—putting on my shoes—and promptly peed squarely in the middle of my back.

Until her dying day, 13 years later, Packy never so much as drooled outside of her cat box. This wasn't an accident. This was an editorial comment on where she figured I fit in the pecking order of the world.

Just a couple of weeks back one of my two current cats in residence took a moment to establish, yet again, what flavor of critter is in charge of Casa Aylworth. Koi is a multi-colored, spayed female kitty, who like all of her species, knows exactly who's in charge. I came upstairs to my bedroom and found Koi half-way up the front of my bureau with a paw clawing up to her furry shoulder in one of the drawers. Like any other male, I have substantial objections to some critter clawing around inside my drawers, so I gave Koi a gently-applied toe of my shoe to remove her from her perch.

Koi meowed out her outrage at my impertinence, but foolishly thinking the topic was closed, I ignored her.

About an hour later, Susan and I were in the living room. My dear bride teaches at the local university and she was grading papers with her briefcase sitting open on the floor. Suddenly the room was filled with somewhat muffled Koi meows as the cat stomped in carrying in her mouth a small, fabric holster used for a flashlight. She literally spat out her burden into Susan's brief case. Then she looked up at me and delivered an unmistakable feline tongue lashing. I didn't really get it until I realized the holster had come out of the drawer where I had caught Koi earlier.

"I can get anything I want, anytime I want it, chubby," she squeaked before stomping back out of the room.

Another cat, Spats, and the then household dog, Oso, taught me cats and dog can share thoughts as well.

Spats, a fixed tom cat, was in his usual perch on the couch when Oso walked up and in a friendly gesture licked the cat's head. Spats responded with a three-second flurry of cat claws around the dog's nose. Oso, apparently stunned by the cat's response, stepped back a pace and shook his head. Then, to the terror of all the two-legs in the room, Oso stepped forward and took Spats' entire head into his cavernous mouth. For three breathless beats Oso held the cat's head like that. Then he opened his mouth and began licking Spats' head again.

Spats had clearly gotten the "I lick it or you lose it" message and stood still while the canine tongued his fur. From that moment, Oso made a point of licking Spats "hello" every time they met, and the cat never once objected.

Communication is a wonderful thing.

● ● ● ●

Hamster Attack!

In the big world of things, how significant is a rodent?

Think about these tiny creatures: a bit of fur, a few ounces of flesh. If they are really being nasty, maybe a good dose of the Black Death, but for the most part they are nothing more than nuisances that scamper away when you flick on the light, but that isn't always the case.

Enter Flashy.

Flashy is a rodent, more specifically a hamster, who belongs to a set of widgets who are both near and dear to me. The widgets in question will remain nameless so the insurance adjuster won't get wise.

Flashy didn't have much to recommend her as a pet. She couldn't sit up, fetch or even roll over and play dead, but her small masters loved her. However, she did have an unexpected talent. This little hamster turned out to be something of an escape artist.

On the night of the disaster, Flashy broke out. The daddy of the widgets swears there is a place in the cage where the bars have been bent apart in your standard Superman-versus-steel-bars routine. The rodent marauder made good her escape at about the same time the household had all settled down to a long winter's nap.

Flashy was a hamster on a mission, and her mission was sabotage.

Jumping ahead a few hours, Daddy awakened to what he thought was the sound of rain on the roof. It sounded like the sky had just opened up and the downpour was impressive. With his eyes barely open he staggered into the kitchen, and found it inches deep in water.

A flood, rolling out from behind the dishwasher, had inundated the kitchen, swamped the laundry room, and was in the process of flushing out the garage.

It took Daddy a couple of minutes to discover the flood was due to a hole in the hose that fed the dishwasher.

On further inspection the gap in the hose looked very like the bite of—ta-duh!—a hamster. Then a search of Flashy's cell revealed her escape.

For the moment Daddy was more interested in flood control than rodenticide. The flood warped the floor, and effectively destroyed the cabinets. To make matters worse these cabinets were all glued together as a unit, which meant none could be replaced without tearing out all of the others.

The chubby checked brown and white hamster, who previously had seemed too intellectually challenged to successfully run on the wheel in her cage, had done thousands of dollars worth of damage, and then vanished like a bad dream.

Dad called his insurance agent who explained ruptured pipes are covered by his homeowner's policy and except for the deductible, the company would cover the repairs.

However, in the interim the family that includes Mom, Dad and three widgets, one being a micro-widget in arms, had to live without a kitchen.

But justice had had its day. Flashy apparently had washed away with her flood, or so Daddy thought.

The next day the blue-eyed, dimple-cheeked apple of her Daddy's eye, made a thrilling discovery?

Flashy had survived and was hiding under the family room couch! Squealing with delight, she joyfully carried Flashy to where Daddy could join in the celebration of the rodent's return.

Thinking that snatching the beast from her daughter's hand, and stomping it into oblivion in the middle of the living room rug, might emotionally scar the little darling for life, Daddy managed to restrain his more violent instincts.

Flashy was returned to her cage, apparently happy to be over her adventure.

The pried-open bars have been repaired, and to hear Daddy there is a reasonable chance the cage will be enhanced with an outer electrified fence, and a very small minefield.

In the long run, Daddy's dear wife will essentially get a new kitchen out of the rodent raid, and the bite from the family pocket will be more easily manageable than was the nip in the water hose.

As for Flashy, for the moment she is alive and well, but tomorrow is another day.

● ● ● ●

Tragedy of substance abuse hits home

One of the great challenges of modern life is the omnipresent scourge of substance abuse. Sadly, even the Aylworth Clan—which is perfect in every way and odor free—has not escaped the evil snare of mind-altering chemicals.

Two of the youngest members of my household are captives to a common weed. They are addicted to *nepeta cataria lamiaceae*! Yes it's true! Our resident felines are utter slaves to catnip!

About four years ago, my dear bride, the saintly Susan, and I adopted a tiny brother-sister team. The plan had been to open our hearts to one homeless kitten, but it was clear from the minute we met these two in the animal shelter that Kola and Koi were inseparable.

Kola, an orange male, and Koi, a calico cat with a serious attitude, became fixtures around the homestead, doing kitten things in the most charming way.

When Susan and I were on one of our weekly pilgrimages to the supermarket, on an impulse I grabbed a catnip mouse off the shelf thinking the cats might enjoy it.

At first the feline pair were tentative about the herb-filled fabric mouse, but then with a rush they went wild. They tossed the "mouse" into the air, and thundered—yes, even with little cat feet they thundered—in reckless disregard for anything but their catnip fix. Susan and I laughed out loud as the little beasts careened into the kitchen, lost traction on the wooden floor, and smacked rump first into the refrigerator.

In due time Koi and Kola carefully tossed the mouse under the couch, where they seem to store everything. The pandemonium came to an abrupt halt, as the exhausted, furry drug fiends slipped off to the top of the couch to rest up.

The problem was I didn't fully appreciate the depth of personal degradation to which my little cat buddies would tumble. Unaware and innocent, I purchased more "mice." Eventually, I was buying them in packs of 10. Susan in her own gentle way bought packets of pure catnip, which the felines would roll in with delusional abandon.

At first it was all fun and games. I suspect Kola and Koi spent time telling each other they didn't have a problem and could quit anytime they wanted to, but they just didn't want to. Slowly things got worse. Instead of waiting for one of their people to toss them a spiked mouse, they began to beg for more. The mournful meows echoed through Casa Aylworth.

We keep the mice in the drawer next to the one that holds the aspirin and antacids. I guess the feline addicts can smell the stash in the adjacent drawer. Every time either of us goes for an aspirin, the druggie duo is there on their hind legs reaching up to the drawer pathetically begging for a catnip fix.

At present the pair haven't figured out how to get into the catnip drawer on their own. I don't think Kola will ever make that intellectual leap, but Koi is a clever little beastie. I'm sure she spends much of the time she pretends to be sleeping actually scheming how she will make the heist. Heck, if Koi had an opposable thumb, she would probably stage a coup and take over the whole house.

I suppose we could just toss the offending weed in the trash, but how would our beloved kitties respond to cold-turkey catnip withdrawal? On the other hand, if we keep feeding their habit, how long will it be until they graduate to locoweed? What's next? Brewing dandelion wine in the garage? When will the madness stop?

● ● ● ●

'I'm sorry. My cat ate your paper'

For something over a quarter century my dear bride, the saintly Susan, has worked as an instructor at the local university. Not surprisingly, at least not to me, Susan is a fabulous teacher, dedicated to helping her students not only to learn but to grow.

Most of her time has been spent teaching what used to be called freshman composition. Now it is officially "academic writing," but it is still about helping students who think text messages are actually English, to learn to communicate with the real written word.

The only way one learns to write is by writing and the only way one's writing can improve is by getting constructive criticism from an instructor skilled in using the language. As a published novelist and playwright, Susan writes with a skill and splendor that often leaves me breathless, and that capacity to write wonderfully prods her to do everything possible to teach and guide her students.

That also means Susan spends endless evening hours grading veritable mountains of student papers. For the majority of those years, Susan shared her home workspace with a collection of widgets who called her "Mom," and that sometimes led to complications.

When our Paul, now a married man on the teetering verge of graduating from college, was in single digits, he had a passionate love for crayons and papers. Sometimes the desire to create his latest Crayola masterpiece struck when there was no art paper in sight. No worries. The stack of white paper on the dinner table would provide him a suitable canvas.

As a result, from time to time, Susan was occasionally forced to explain to one of her students why there were green mountains and purple flowers decorating his or her essay on the future of American education. Since most kids have siblings, they usually took the juvenile artwork on their papers in stride. Eventually we either convinced Paul to ask for paper, or he grew out of his Crayola phase. Either way the essay adornments ended.

Sometimes it wasn't the resident widgets, but the lateness of the grading hour that left Susan's students wondering. Susan always writes detailed critiques on her students' papers, praising the good things they accomplished, and pointing out specific deficiencies they still needed to address. Her dedication and attention to detail sometimes means the grading sessions stretch into the wee hours of the morning.

One day after she had returned a load of graded papers, an apparently befuddled member of Susan's class had a concern. "Mrs. Aylworth, I'm not sure I understand this comment," asked the student, handing back the paper. At the top of the essay, written in Susan's beautiful, fluid script, was a note that read, "Be aware of comma faults and the Big Bad Wolf."

After the last word the note trailed off in a ragged line. Not wanting to admit that she had fallen asleep in mid comment, Susan said something like, "Of course you have to watch out for the Big Bad Wolf! There are lots of dangerous characters on this campus!"

Humans are not the only ones to have an impact on student papers. In our current world, Susan and I share our domicile with a dog and two cats, none of whom like to use crayons. However, that doesn't mean that four-legged weirdness is out of the question.

The other evening I came home after a late work assignment and there was Susan at the kitchen counter poring over student papers. As she worked, our calico cat, Koi, leapt to the counter and proceeded to sit on the pile of papers. Then for reasons known only to Koi's walnut-size brain, she began methodically to lick the paper she was sitting on.

"Great!" said Susan in exasperation. "I can just hear myself trying to explain, 'I'm sorry but my cat ate your paper.' I wouldn't believe that. Why should they?"

She then bopped Koi on her tail, and the cat jumped off the counter. A few cat lick marks won't be noticed and, if they are, Susan will come up with an amazing explanation. Either way, she will continue to bless her students with her wisdom and her creativity.

● ● ● ●

The elephant in the living room

My dear darling grandwidget, Sydnie, gave me one of those looks that says, "My grandpa is a nut case!"

Getting that look from Sydnie isn't all that rare for me. This little blonde cherub is four going on 16, and even at her tender age she has discovered that ol' grandpa tends to skip to the beat of his own drummer.

But it wasn't my original announcement that made her wonder about my sanity.

"Grandma and I are getting an elephant."

"Where ya gonna keep it, Grandpa?"

"In the living room of our new house."

It never crossed Sydnie's mind to scoff at the notion of owning an elephant.

Even though Casa Aylworth III, which is in the building process, sits in the middle of a subdivision on a small city lot, the idea of a pet pachyderm apparently sounded entirely reasonable to her 4-year-old mind, but in the house?

"Grandpa, you can't keep a elephant in the living room!"

"Why not?"

I watched fascinated as Sydnie tried to wrap her charming little mind around the question of why elephants don't belong indoors. At some level she knew as a given that it was a bad idea, but explaining why was a tough question.

Then her bright blue eyes gleamed with new understanding. She had the absolute answer. "Elephants are messy. Grandma will get real mad at you!"

In point of fact my dear bride, the saintly Susan, is a full, if not entirely thrilled, conspirator in the elephant caper.

The road to an elephant in the living room began about three years ago when Susan and I decided to sell the original Casa Aylworth, the feeble little hovel where we raised all seven of our widgets.

The deal we worked out meant that the day would come when the old place would be torn down, we would move into an interim house, and finally move to the grand palace that will be Casa Aylworth III. OK, it won't be a palace, but it is such an upgrade from the previous digs that just thinking about the place makes my head spin.

Now CA3 is close to completion and Susan and I have been prowling furniture stores looking for the perfect things to fill our new home. For most of our lives we have had to decorate based on what was cheap and built tough enough to survive seven very active small people. Tubular steel frames with heavy canvas upholstery tended to be the norm. On average our furniture had the grace and charm of an army cot.

With the advent of CA3, we are no longer merely buying furniture. We can in fact decorate. Susan takes lead in this effort, because frankly, I have no taste. I would mix stripes and plaids, paint adjacent walls in different day-glow colors, and decorate with orange crates and gas station signs if left to my own devices.

We've purchased a Persian rug, love seats and sofas, a mammoth canopy bed, huge mirrors, sectionals, recliners, and a six-piece, antique, red velvet-covered settee set for the formal parlor.

For the most part my role in this has been to say, "If that's what you want, Susan, it's great with me," and, thank goodness, I mean it.

Then during one of our forays into a furniture store, I saw an elephant. The mini beast is about 4 feet tall to the tip of its upraised trunk and just about the same in length. It has no value. It doesn't light up. It doesn't have a radio in its belly and it won't even trumpet at intruders. It just stands there.

I was elephant-smitten at first sight.

Susan, who mostly appreciates the strange little boy that lives inside her allegedly adult husband, graciously agreed to my flight of fancy. So for whimsy's sake, we are becoming elephant owners. Yes, Sydnie, there will be an elephant in the living room, and if it's messy, I'm on imaginary dung duty.

● ● ● ●

Possums of the Undead

As a resurrection should, this started just before dawn on a Sunday morning.

I had an early meeting that day and was in the process of heading for the door when my two resident canines—Che and Pirate—began barking and growling, which is rare for these two.

After shouting the obligatory "SHADDUP!" out the window, I felt compelled to investigate. As I stepped onto the back patio, I discovered a large—five pound—and decidedly dead possum lying on the concrete.

There was no time for a traditional backyard funeral, so donning a pair of rubber gloves, I took the recently departed and still warm critter by the tail and dropped him in a nice new garbage bag, and dumped it in the empty garbage can—THUMP!

Exit Roger to his meeting.

About 12 hours later I was about to dump some normal trash into the can, but when I opened the lid, the "dead" possum was no longer in the plastic bag. He was still lying on his side and absolutely motionless, but this time a very black eye was open and seemed to be staring at me.

Then I did what I always do when confronted by the undead. I ran back in the house yelling for Susan. After a two-second peek into the garbage can, Susan declared the possum resurrected. Yes I had heard the phrase "playing possum," but if there is an academy award for possum performances, this marsupial had it nailed. He never so much as twitched as I picked him up and dropped him in the bag.

Now that he was back from the dead, we were left with the immediate challenge of how to set him free. Susan asked if I had some thick gloves, to which I responded, "Are you out of your mind?"

Then a bright idea erupted. I have a post-hole digger. Maybe I could —very gently—use the clamshell end to grab the beast to set him free.

Any lingering doubt the possum was in fact among the living was wiped out the instant he saw the tool descending into the can. Teeth bared and hissing, the critter explained this was a really bad plan.

Proving I can ultimately grasp the obvious, I realized the thing to do was open the gate to the outside world and tip over the can to set the beastie loose.

I dumped him out on the concrete. After the day this possum had had, I figured he'd beat feet the heck out of Dodge the minute he was free, but he just shuffled a few feet out of the gate and stopped.

His lack of a hasty exit made me worry about him. After all, he'd been intimidated by a pair of giant carnivorous monsters, Pirate and Che. Then a two-legged creature had grabbed him by the tail, tied him into an airtight plastic bag, dropped it into a dark, stinky, ragingly hot box, and on top of everything else—he'd been "dead" all day. Maybe he could use some water?

Susan agreed, but her efforts to get water for the beleaguered critter startled him and he tried to duck under the gate back into the yard, getting stuck under it in the process. This possum was having a really bad day.

Very gingerly—the critter was again showing off his nifty teeth—I reopened the gate, freeing him, and the minute he was released he trotted, a bit more swiftly, toward me. This was a choice I wanted to discourage, so I stamped my feet and said something witty like, "No! No! No!"

He reversed course but again stopped just outside the gate. Hoping to encourage his total escape, I continued to stomp my size 12s on the concrete. To my relief he scampered, well at least strolled, around the corner of the house and out of sight. By the time I shut the gate and went around front to see where he had gone—POOF!—no possum. I searched but never found a sign of him again, which I guess is appropriate for a creature which had just come back from the dead.

Resident felines prove cats can chat

I was standing in the shower when suddenly I had a "Psycho" moment. I could 'feel' somebody looking at me. I turned, expecting to find Norman Bates' mommy standing in the door, and sure enough I had a spectator.

Koi, one of a set of unlikely fraternal twin kitties that let us share Casa Aylworth III, was staring fixedly at me in the shower. I'm sure, from a cat's point of view, deliberately standing in a stream of hot water seems more than a bit odd.

I believe in cross-species communication, so standing there, naked and dripping, I explained to Koi that this is how I got clean. I told her if I tried to lick myself clean, like she and her brother, Kola, do, I'd throw up. I suspect that logic didn't carry much weight with Koi, because she and her brother apparently think there is nothing unusual about erupting hair-balls around the household.

While being stared at by the cat while in the shower can be a bit unnerving, I do enjoy chats with my felines. What makes it more fun is the cats answer me when we talk.

Oh, I understand there are those misguided and ill informed souls who don't recognize that cats—and a whole bunch of other critters, for that matter—not only understand speech but can communicate quite successfully.

There are times when Koi or Kola meow at me, and I know precisely what they are saying. Koi, for example, has developed something of a scheduled communication with my dear bride, the saintly Susan. Some time around sunset every day, Koi seeks out Susan and begins to chatter. While to the inexperienced it may sound like the meaningless mewings of a critter with a brain the size of an anemic walnut, to Susan the message is crystal clear.

"OK!" says Koi, "It's time you notice me! I want you to come into the garage with me and acknowledge the obvious fact that my food bowl needs immediate attention!!!"

Really Koi acts like any small child, and we have come to believe these two have the thinking capacity of slightly slow 3-year-olds. Like a 3-year-old, Koi doesn't tend to check conditions before making demands. As often as not the complaining feline already has a full food bowl, but Koi will not be mollified until her human has checked.

Kola, as befits even an altered tomcat, is more inclined to recline than demand, with one great exception.

Koi and Kola are litter-mates. They demonstrably have the same mother, but she was . . . well . . . free with her affections and our two cats clearly have different daddies. Kola is half again bigger than his sister, and bright orange, while Koi is colored like a finger painter's smock.

I'm not sure Kola fully recognizes that he and Koi are separate beasts. That becomes an issue because Koi is the more adventurous of the two and she bolts out the door from time to time. Kola apparently figures the world inside the walls is much to be preferred, but when Koi disappears, he gets frantic. He usually seeks me out to report, "My other half is missing!!!"

I explain to him his sister is a thoughtless twit and she will come home because we own the food bowl.

When Koi does return home, Kola reads her a feline riot act, meowing about how mean it is for her to put him through this torture and punctuating his complaint with a sharp nip or two.

That usually ends with Koi beating the snot out of her much bigger brother. Susan and I avoid interfering in these domestic disputes. We both know the siblings will seek us out eventually to tell us all about it.

Mechanical Monsters

Mah truck is more than just wheels

Would you forgive me if I indulged in a little overt gloating?

I have THE COOLEST TRUCK IN THE WHOLE, ENTIRE WORLD!!!

For my birthday, my dear bride, the saintly Susan, and the whole entire crowd of Aylworth widgets and grandwidgets surprised me—read that totally blew me away—when they presented me with a brand new, four-door pickup.

This is the second time in my life my dear bride has given me a vehicle for a present, but this is the first time in all my years that I have ever owned a new, as in it had 24 miles on the odometer, vehicle that was mine.

It has had a serious effect on my psyche.

For most of my life a vehicle has been transportation. It was a way to get from point A to B. They have never been a source of ego enhancement. The cars I have owned have been autos I could afford. I felt like I had achieved a certain level of success when I purchased an auto that was made in the same decade that I bought it. They have been mechanic's delights, running more on faith and prayer than vehicular prowess, and as often as not they proved my faith was weak.

I have spent my driving career parking in inconspicuous places to give me a chance to deny connection to the ambulating collection of loosely associated rolling piles of used parts. The vehicles were old, wrinkled, and usually green. If they did anything for my sense of self, it was to help keep me humble.

Then all of a sudden there is this big, shiny, powerful, **MANLY** truck in my driveway. This chariot has seats that don't sag, and an engine that roars into life on command.

It has an air conditioner that will create icicles as I drive through the devil's backyard, and it has these big, black protectors around the front and the wheel-wells, that look like armor plate that has been bolted on. On top of everything else, the official name of the color of my baby is "Granite." Now, how cool is that??!!

I find myself rolling down the street feeling sorry for the little people who aren't driving a pickup as cool as mine. I smile—patronizingly—at the teen-agers as they drive by in their muscle cars. I make mental fun of the person in the luxury sedan ahead of me, who is driving around with her turn signal on. My truck wouldn't do that.

If I meet a stranger my first question is, "Wanna come see my truck?"

When I say "truck," I find my voice drops into the lower, more manly registers.

It isn't just "my truck." It is absolutely "**MAH TRUCK!!!**"

It has changed my entire world view. I have gone from "Roger, mild-mannered-reporter-for-a-really-nice-medium-sized-newspaper," to "ROGER!! PICKUP-DRIVER-GUY-WHO IS A MILD-MANNERED-REPORTER-FOR-A-VIBRANT-PULSE-POUNDING-REALLY-NICE-MEDIUM-SIZED-NEWSPAPER!"

At some level, I have turned into a 16-year-old boy. I want to drive everywhere. I'll drive my trash can from the house to the curb, and then drive the empty can back to the house. And the cab still even smells new! I can't stand it!!

●　　●　　●　　●

Automotive Flirtation Takes Me to World of COOL

He handed me the keys and I was immediately convinced he had made a big mistake.

I was making a rush trip to attend the university graduation of my dear daughter-in-law, Carly, and since time was an important issue, I flew. Step Two of my travel plans had me at the rental car counter waiting to pick up the econo-box I had reserved.

The "sub-compacts" I always rent are inherently cramped, ugly and boring, but they get my posterior from point A to point B without me having to walk. The pleasant young man behind the counter handed me the keys and explained, "Your silver Mustang convertible is in slot K-7."

I can be pretty slow on the uptake, but the words "Mustang" and "convertible" immediately got my attention.

"You think a Mustang is a 'sub-compact' car?" I asked.

"No, sir. I think a Mustang is a sports car, but it is all we have available right now and we will charge you the sub-compact rate."

I expected this adventure in automotive fantasy was going to go 'poof!,' but when I found K-7, there sat a brand new, gleaming, metallic silver, convertible Mustang!

While my best vehicular buddy—"MAH TRUCK," which was a birthday gift from my dear bride, the saintly Susan—is the joy of my automotive life, I have had a crush on Mustangs since I was one.

During my high school years—1965 to 1968—the Mustang was the epitome of cool and that was made even more so because our school mascot was also the Mustang. For three years I was a LINCOLN MUSTANG!

It was way too dark and way too cold for any sane person to be driving around in a convertible, so naturally I had the top down as I roared onto the freeway. After a few minutes behind the wheel, I was at my in-laws' home, where I would be staying during my visit. I really wanted to just drive around for a bit longer, but I consoled myself with the knowledge the Mustang was going to be mine for three whole days.

My severe case of vehicular infatuation didn't keep the pessimistic side of my soul from kicking in. The last time I visited my in-laws, while driving a truly under-powered and unimpressive rented econo-box, I was stopped for speeding. I was doing 23 in a 20-mile-per-hour zone. While I was let off with a warning, I had reason to believe the local cops were on the fanatic end of serious about enforcing the speed laws. The problem was the Mustang looked like it was doing 90 while it was still parked.

Throwing caution to the wind, the next morning I surrendered to this mechanical hottie's charms. With the top down, my shades in place, and the oldies radio station blaring "American Pie"—"A long, long time ago . . . I can still remember how that music used to make me smile"—I was cruising.

A young guy in a pickup drove by and shouted "Love your car!" I waved back in humble acknowledgment of the obvious. I was officially and undeniably cool.

While being truly obsessive about adhering to the speed laws, I showed this car off shamelessly. I took Carly, and her husband, my son, Paul, on an entirely unjustified spin around town just to let people envy me and my rented status. I even got my father- and mother-in-law in it, my Mom-in-law in the front seat and my Dad-in-law in the back.

The back seat in this car was pretty much a mirage. Oh there is a back seat and there is plenty of leg-room as long as you are no taller than 2-foot-8, but I think my father-in-law got a kick out of the car despite having his knees stuck firmly in his ears.

In passing I thought somebody might think the old guy in the cool car is obviously suffering a mid-life crisis, but I rejected that out of hand. After all, I'm 56, so for this to be a mid-life crisis, I'd have to live to 112, which doesn't seem too likely.

As such flings do, the days with the Mustang came to an end. I turned the car in at the airport and flew home where my beloved spouse and MAH TRUCK waited to welcome me.

I will never own a Mustang. In my world they just aren't practical, but when I am old and gray—yeah! OK! I am old and gray, but when I am much older and grayer—I will recall the three-day flirtation and remember the wind in my hair and the sunburn on my nose, and how for a wee moment in time, I was cool!

● ● ● ●

Monster alarm beeps away sleep

Since I was a high school kid I have been an early riser.

Initially I had special classes that required I be up and at the world while the roosters were still in Snoozeville. In college I worked as a 4 a.m. janitor. When I got into the professional world my jobs have generally forced me into the pre-dawn patrol. The net result is I have seen a lot of wonderful sunrises over the last four decades. All of that is well and good, but I have a problem.

I really hate getting up before the sun.

As a result I luxuriate in those days when I can sleep in. Most Saturdays, but not all, I can blissfully turn off the alarm and stay cozily ensconced in Dreamland. On a recent Friday night I was looking forward to just such a Saturday morning. The very last thing I said to Susan before drifting off to the land of nod was, "I've turned off the alarm."

Then I was attending a Cowsills concert—don't ask me to explain that. I was, after all, sound asleep at the time—when for some reason the band included this annoying "BEEP-BEEP-BEEP" in the song. After a few seconds the concert disappeared into a foggy level of consciousness, but the blasted "BEEP-BEEP-BEEPING" kept its annoying cadence.

I looked at my alarm clock which was sitting silently by the side of the bed. The clock said it was 4:20 a.m., but it was decidedly not the source of the beeps. The noise was coming in through the window and when enough of the fog cleared, I thought I recognized it as the beep that a large piece of construction equipment makes when it backs up. There is home construction going on all around Casa Aylworth, but nobody is out playing on a bulldozer at 4 in the freaking morning!

I waited for a few minutes, thinking foolishly the backing up would end and the beeping would die, but it didn't. I shut the window, but the persistent beeping seemed to come through the very walls. I crawled out of bed, more or less dressed, grabbed my camera and a flashlight, and went in search of the evil beeper.

I was going to find this thing, get a picture complete with licenses, company names, and the face of the human driving the wretched thing, then I was going to call in the police.

I wandered through the neighborhood, trying to zero in on the sound. I had gone three blocks when I finally found the offending road grader, sitting alone and totally unloved in the middle of a construction site. No humans were around, and the machine wasn't backing up because it wasn't even turned on, but it was sure enough beeping.

I was shooting pictures and considering arson as a secondary approach to the problem, when I spotted a police officer driving by. I flagged him down. Crazy, half-dressed, 55-year-old men flailing their arms like windmills tend to attract cops fairly quickly. He asked if I had made the noise complaint, which to my chagrin I had not, but I led him to the culprit.

The officer, who by then had decided I was harmless, said he would try to identify the owner. Failing that, the cop said he would try to disengage the battery to silence the obviously defective beeper.

I said if he wanted to shoot the wretched thing, I wouldn't tell. Seeing how the situation was in better—and armed—hands, I headed home. Before I got back to the homestead the beeping ceased. I don't know how the officer accomplished the deed, but everything up to and including mechanical mayhem was fine with me.

With the world's biggest alarm finally silenced, I went back to bed, but I never did go back to the Cowsills concert.

I hate alarms!

●　●　●　●

New gizmo brings blessed reversal of fortune

When it comes to building things, repairing things, assembling things, or just about any other behavior or practice that requires the use of tools, I'm pretty much a disaster waiting to happen.

Hand tools are uniformly not my friends. Hammers tend to attack my fingers at random. Screwdrivers gouge some wonderful holes in my hands, and let's not even talk about power tools.

That's why when I announced I was going to undertake a project involving tools, my dear bride, the saintly Susan, immediately tried to talk me out of it.

For Christmas, Susan bought me a back-up camera, which isn't an additional camera to have around if my good one breaks. It is a camera I attached to the rear of my pickup to help me see what's sneaking up from behind.

The incredibly cool vehicle that I call MAH TRUCK is a personal friend of mine, a fact that is not lost on Susan.

So when I announced my intention to wire something to the electrical system of MAH TRUCK, and to affix a camera to the rear and a tiny television screen to the dashboard, my bride was . . . ah . . . er . . . well, skeptical.

But this time I faked her out. I actually read the instructions—three times as a matter of fact—and I was convinced this job was within my admittedly small skill zone. I also immediately knew I was going to ignore some of the instructions.

The concept that I might ignore instructions doesn't come as a particular surprise to Susan. She knows how I attack a baking project and accepts as a given that I view a recipe as more of set of a suggestions than absolute requirements.

In this case the electronic recipe wanted me to wire the camera to the backup lights, so I could only see things on my little screen when I was in fact backing up. If you can only use your backup camera when you are in fact backing up, what's the fun in that? I wanted to be able to see where I've been even while I was going somewhere else.

So instead of using power from the backup lights, I wired my wee little camera into the light that illuminates my license plate. The miniature monitor is plugged into the cigarette lighter for power and mounted on my dashboard. The little monitor has a wireless receiver and the camera on the bumper sends the rearview pictures by radio signal to the screen.

After spending an hour doing what it would take a marginally competent 10-year-old 15 minutes to accomplish, the wiring was all connected and the monitor was mounted. Then came the great test.

While I was absolutely certain-sure I had it all done properly, past experience forced me to consider the possibility I would fry my automotive buddy's entire electrical system when I switched the camera on.

Under the heading of nothing ventured, nothing gained, I turned on the lights and the monitor.

Instantly the monitor fluttered to life and I was gazing at a 3 1/2-inch square view of my garage, in living color no less.

It is so cool. It not only didn't blow up MAH TRUCK, but it performs as advertised.

I'm so thrilled with my new technological prowess that I'm dragging friends, family and total strangers from off the street into the cab of the pickup to show off the monitor.

I've also discovered that in the totality of the driving experience, I spend a fairly brief amount of time going backward, but that's OK. I can turn on the monitor and watch while I'm driving forward.

The only problem is I can't really watch where I'm going all that successfully while staring at my rear view camera.

I think I've come up with a solution to that. I can watch the monitor all I want if I'm willing to drive to places in reverse. It makes perfect sense to me and besides that, it is so cool!

● ● ● ●

A goofy voice in the night repeating "I love you"

Parents understand that an uninterrupted night's sleep is more often a wish than a reality, but I recently learned that for modern young parents there are a whole lot of new voices in the night.

When my widgets were small, there was an impressive collection of electrical toys that could make a truly appalling noise. I particularly remember a "constant action" police car that I made the mind-numbing mistake of giving to my senior son, Aaron, for his third birthday. Once turned on, this beast erupted in a cacophony of raging sirens and roaring engine sounds as it careened around the floor, lights flashing.

Inexplicably the batteries ran out on the car almost instantly. Sadly—for Aaron—the D-cell batteries needed for his car suddenly went off the market and could never be purchased again. Once the power was cut on the car, silence returned.

That's how things were back in the good old days, clear back in the last century. You turned off a toy and that was it. It was inert. That apparently is no longer guaranteed.

The other day I was complaining to my son Adam about how I had unsuccessfully, I thought, attempted to sign on to an Internet connection to a San Francisco radio station. I was trying to listen to a baseball game that wasn't being broadcast locally, but try as I might my computer wouldn't make the hook-up. What I didn't realize was my computer was in an electronic queue waiting patiently for a chance to connect to the station's Web site.

At about 4 the next morning the computer's patience paid off. I was blasted into something approaching consciousness by the sound of a pair of broadcast jocks screaming at each other. They were arguing about the game I never got to hear, but at that hour, and with the brain still largely in a fog, I was convinced the house had been invaded by the loudest and dumbest burglars in the history of nocturnal larceny. On investigation, I discovered the miscreant was my computer and with a punch of a button, peace was restored.

Adam had not the tiniest speck of sympathy for me. He said being awakened from a sound sleep by inexplicable voices was more or less the norm in his household.

Recognizing he has a house full of his own widgets, I wasn't too impressed with his lament until he explained the voices weren't his kids or even human. There was, for example, the night a gruff male voice boomed through the house, shouting, "LET'S GET TO WORK!"

Adam initially thought the voice was his subconscious pounding on the inside of his skull, kicking him about a project he needed to finish, so he muttered, "Let's get to sleep" in response.

When he reached a more complete level of consciousness, Adam got up to investigate, only to discover the demanding voice was coming from a toy skip-loader that hadn't been entirely turned off.

On a fairly regular basis, Adam is awakened in the dark of the night by a goofy voice repeating, "I love you; you love me." In that case the culprit is an inane, purple dinosaur with a defective circuit.

On the other end of the spectrum is an electrical cheetah. When it gets wet, and small children have no problem providing a range of ways to make a toy wet, the off button becomes more of a suggestion than a command. Suddenly an apparently drug-crazed voice echoes through the night, "I want some hot stuff!"

Since Adam is a crack shot, and a heavily armed hunter, I have to assume this cheetah's long-term survival is in great doubt.

While I am button-bustingly proud of the seven extraordinary adults that call me Dad, there are times when I miss the little people they once were. Having said that, I'm not sorry I don't have to deal with a toy demanding, "I want some hot stuff!" when both it and I should be turned off for the night.

● ● ● ●

Vehicular bumpage is reason to be glad wife is away

I generally complain loudly about her absence, when my dear bride the saintly Susan, is out of town, but I recently bumped into a situation that gave me cause to be pleased she's not around.

The thing that I bumped into was a parked car. I was pulling out of my own garage at Casa Aylworth III late one night, and clearly I was not paying adequate attention, when I felt a very mild bump.

The less noble side of my character immediately began lobbying for a quick getaway, but the good angels held sway and I pulled to the side of the road. On checking, I found an undeniable dimple in the driver's side of the victim vehicle.

I've seen the little car parked there many times in the past and I assumed it belonged to one of my next door neighbor's sons. So despite the late hour, I knocked on my neighbor's door. When one of the boys answered, I confessed I had bumped what I suspected was his car.

After a quick discussion he explained it wasn't his vehicle, but it belonged to his buddy who was visiting, and the buddy and I went out to inspect his wounded vehicular comrade. The owner was a pleasant young man, and while he was less than thrilled that some aged moron had smacked his wheeled friend, he handled it with calm patience.

He lovingly stroked the ouch on his car's side. Having suffered a vehicular insult to my own best automotive friend—MAH TRUCK— when a garbage truck backed up into my hood, I fully understood his pain. I provided him the necessary insurance information and heaped a substantial pile of apologies on his head.

While I was talking to the owner, one of my sons who was overnighting at my place with his wife, came out to see what is going on. This particular son, whose name I will keep private to protect both of us, has a long and humorous history of automotive bumpage. In the first hour after he got his driver's license this dear lad managed to smack into a parked car. Within another month, he had backed into a pole in a parking lot that he sincerely swore had just erupted out of the pavement behind him. "Dad it wasn't there! It just wasn't there!"

But on this particular night I was standing out there with my own bumper hanging out and my son looking on. To his credit he didn't say, "Well Dad, how did you not see a parked car?" To which I didn't have to respond, "Son it wasn't there! It just wasn't!"

I also didn't have to explain to my dear bride, who keeps the family books, why our auto insurance is probably going to be climbing in the near future.

Susan is good about such things, and in all fairness the damage I did isn't all that impressive. At least it isn't that impressive to me. The young man who belongs to the car might understandably disagree.

Even so the male ego portion of telling my bride that I apparently am officially dumber than a box of mud is something I can happily avoid, at least for now.

Undoubtedly, she will eventually learn of my automotive misdeed—even good insurance goes only so far—but the opportunity to forestall the inevitable is a gift I can savor for the moment.

In point of fact, Susan won't even be in town when this column appears. So if all of you people will keep your mouths shut when you see her, I'd appreciate it.

● ● ● ●

Trip teaches lessons about chains and survival

When my car decided—all on its own—to make a 90-degree right turn, I realized this might not be a good day. My best friend and dear bride, the saintly Susan, and I had made a brief vacation excursion two states east, and with the holiday coming to an end, we were headed home.

The trip home usually takes us 10 to 12 hours depending on the number of stops we make and how long it takes us to lose the $5 in nickels we have allocated to the slots in Elko. It's a long ride, but Susan and I have discovered traveling in a comfortable and reliable vehicle, without a back seat full of the "are-we-there-yet?!" generation, can be an entirely pleasurable experience.

We'd been on the road about an hour, having discussed and decided how to fix all of the problems in the lives of our family members, and we were well on our way to solving all of the evils of the entire world when the snow began.

Snow is an interesting thing. It's made of water but it can be almost dry, and its postcard beauty can lull the unsuspecting, or the downright stupid, into thinking it is as benign a meteorological event as it appears.

As a native Californian I have relatively little experience with white stuff from the sky, and while it does snow in northeastern Arizona, where Susan grew to maturity, she has been living in a more civilized climate for many years. The net result is we went rolling along just as if we had good sense.

Somewhere out in the geographical center of absolutely nowhere, a sign with a flashing amber light directed us to stop and put on tire chains. I had purchased chains for the car a couple of years back, but never had a reason to take them out of the bag. Suddenly, I'm kneeling in frigid slush by the side of the freeway, with my fingers turning a fascinating shade of pale blue, trying to attach this absurd collection of metal links and cables to my wheels. After an hour of trial and error, with an emphasis on error, I got the chains attached.

With an utterly irrational sense of security, we plunged back down the road.

Within a few miles the freeway climbed into a mountain pass and the snow went from being a charming spectacle to something more akin to a fearful monster.

People with an IQ larger than their hat size know you don't stop in snow unless it is absolutely necessary. So, of course, I decided to stop at the apex of this pass to check and tighten the chains. I was pulling back onto the ice-clad freeway after that stop when gravity went away.

The car made a right-angle turn, throwing us into a pulse-pounding skid. Sliding down the road, with the prospect of sudden violent, death weighing on my fevered mind, two questions took immediate prominence: How much traffic is barreling down on us, and how deep is the snow-covered ditch we are sliding towards? The ditch seemed to be the most immediate concern.

I was taught, way back in high school driver's ed, to never even think about touching the brakes while in a skid. So immediately I mashed down on the suckers, spinning the car another 90 degrees, with the result we came to a stop facing the wrong way in the fast lane. Thankfully there wasn't another vehicle in sight.

Shaken but not stirred, I very, very slowly turned the car back around and continued west at a pace that would not have impressed a 3-year-old on a tricycle. I was pretty much at the mindless-babbling stage, when after nine hours on the road, we pulled into Winnemucca, the spot we consider halfway in our normal drive.

A surviving element of good sense, accompanied with a suspicion that doom lurked at the western border of the town, prompted me to suggest we stop for the night. I think Susan would have knocked me down and tied me to a lamp post if I had tried to drive on, so she greeted my stopover suggestion with instant ascent. The next day dawned sunny and beautiful and the rest of the trip was made with essentially uneventful ease.

This trip was an important learning experience for me. I understand that chains don't necessarily mean cars will drive straight. Most importantly I've learned, during winter if the total trip distance is farther than I can throw a Buick, in the future we fly.

● ● ● ●

Background music could make life easier

When I have nothing important to keep my mind occupied—which seems to be a surprisingly large percentage of the time—I let the poor thing wander, and I'm truly afraid it is not big enough to be out by itself.

On one of these more recent unmonitored brain wanderings, I came up with a really cool idea. Wouldn't life be a whole lot more fun, and safer, if it came with background music?

I'm not talking about having my own personal elevator music

tracks. With the advent of a wide range of electronic recording devices, I can provide music to wander around with me any time I want. What I have in mind isn't just portable tunes. I want the sort of theatrical background music that dances, sometimes unnoticed, behind the action on the movie screen.

Think about it.

You step out of the front door on the way to work, and all of a sudden you can hear Uncle Rhemus singing, "Zippidy doo dah, zippidy yea. My, oh my, what a wonderful day!" and you know without checking this is going to be a really good day.

Then it's sunny, and you are tooling down an utterly straight, totally empty freeway, and the flying music from the movie "Top Gun" begins to ring through the car. It is clearly a message from the great beyond that this is the day to find out if the new car really, truly can break the land speed record, and there will be no payback to ruin the triumph.

On the other end of the spectrum, it's a pitch black night. Heavy rains are pelting down. You've been driving all day and the only thing that is keeping you from falling asleep at the wheel is the sure knowledge there is a tree in this soggy forest just waiting to leap out in front of your car. Then like an oasis in the desert, an electric motel sign, with the word "vacancy" displayed, looms into welcome sight.

You park and dash into the lobby. Behind the counter is a sallow young man wearing the name tag, "Norman." He greets you. As the background music comes up, you hear those eerie, "eek! eek! eek!" violin tones, and you run screaming to your car before Norman's mommy pops out.

It's a party. You didn't want to go. You thought this might be a better night to dust your butterfly collection, but somehow you went. At the other side of the crowded room you see her, just as the strains of "Some Enchanted Evening" begin playing in your head.

Before you make it across the room, you've already picked out names for your 2.3 children. You haven't even met her yet, but you know how it will end.

It's a lovely day at the seaside. After slathering yourself with enough sun screen to protect yourself form a thermonuclear blast, you head toward the surf. As you touch the water you hear, faintly at first, "Da-duh! Da-duh!" in the background. As you wade in a little deeper the music "Da-Duh! Da-duh!" is coming louder and faster. A vision of a massive shark fin slicing through the waves comes to mind, and you run—do not walk—to the nearest dry land, deciding a vacation in the mountains would be a much better choice this season.

Okay, so there is very little chance theatrical background music will ever become a universal companion, but cell phones were a product of Dick Tracy-type science fiction until they showed up in everybody's pocket, so who knows? Until it happens, I can hum to myself and pretend.

● ● ● ●

Stepping into new cell phone adventure

While I have no talent, and very little knowledge, when it comes to things technological, I am, and suspect I will always be, a heartfelt fan of gadgets and gizmos. Given the opportunity, the budget, and the absolute assurance my dear bride the saintly Susan, would never find out, I fear I would buy every device Ron Popeil ever featured on an info-mercial.

Having said that, I have an ongoing fascination—even if it is something of a love-hate relationship—with cell phones.

I come from the days when you could have any kind of telephone you wanted as long as it was black, had a dial, and weighed a ton. The phone had two purposes. You could make and receive calls and the heavy beast made a great paperweight.

It was also a time when the coolest show on television, Star Trek—the first one—featured these great little communicators you could flip open when you wanted talk to somebody: "Beam me up, Scotty!"

I still view cell phones as essentially science fiction made real. I resisted getting one of the new-fangled things for a long time, but long distance travel and a desire to keep my out-of-state widgets on an electronic leash prompted me to take the plunge.

My first tentative step into the wonderful new world of electronic communication was pretty much a failure. I bought a phone and signed up for a two-year contract with a company that had nifty ads, but their phones only worked if you were standing under a cell tower, and then only on alternate Thursdays.

I really flipped out when the company told me the cell phone I had purchased for my darling daughter, Rebecca, and over which I had talked to her many times over a two-month period, didn't exist. When I showed them the listing of my daughter's cell phone number on my phone's bill, they told me it was a "technical anomaly," which meant, "We don't care what the facts are. We say we're right."

Ultimately it turned out the company had given Rebecca's phone number to another client and when he started getting bills for her service, he canceled and her phone number went "poof."

After that fiasco I did more research before I hooked up with another cell phone company and this time I got one that provided pretty good service, but that was about three years ago. When it comes to this flavor of technology, three years ago is effectively the dark ages. The phone I got then is just above flint knives and bear skin clothing on the electronic evolutionary scale.

My phone won't take pictures, download ring tones, provide

global positioning, open garage doors or defrost tonight's dinner. It is just "so last year!" However, trying to catch up, get with it, or be in fashion has never been one of my strong suits. A colleague of mine, a charming, intelligent and witty person, who is the only individual on a planet who can walk around the newsroom barefoot and get away with it, once told me, "Roger you are tragically unhip!" which is obviously true.

Nonetheless, I'm investigating another foray into cell phones. I'm not sure I want one that takes pictures. The company has a set of these camera phones and the only pictures I have successfully taken with them are of the inside of my pants pocket.

A phone that would tell me where I am and how to get where I want to be would be cool, but the coolest will be when I get one that will let me talk to Scotty and Capt. Kirk.

● ● ● ●

Squaring Off for a Fight with the Calendar

Squaring off for a fight with the calendar

Between the calendar, my now silvery hair color, and a collection of widgets who keep asking me things like, "Dad, was Genghis Khan really a bad guy?" I'm more or less forced to admit I am in fact getting older.

Those same children—my own offspring who allegedly love me—are of the fairly loud impression that I am no longer "getting older." They pretty much take the position that I have arrived at old. This opinion is coming from a group of people who think anything that happened before the creation of MTV qualifies as prehistoric.

Regardless of their somewhat myopic vision of what constitutes old, I concede I have been piling on a few years. While I can't do anything about the steady march of days across my calendar, that doesn't mean I have to go quietly to my rocker and begin muttering to invisible visitors.

For a year I've been on a diet and to everybody's surprise, including my own, my hugeness has dropped to the point that now I only weigh as much as a first string defensive end in the NFL, but that is several positive steps down from my high point.

Historically, which means prior to two years ago, I considered climbing two flights of stairs a workout. Taking the garbage to the curb was a project that required days of preparation and other days after the fact to recover. Now I go to the gym on a regular basis. I still pretty much look like a walrus in my work out clothes and I have never gotten to the point where I "enjoy" exercise. There is just nothing about pumping iron—which in my case is a lot more like pressing aluminum foil—or climbing a mechanical staircase that never quite gets to the top, that reaches my standard for pleasurable recreation.

Despite that I keep at it because the alternative—congealing into an immobile mass of trembling tissue—is an option I like even less.

After many months of trying to beat my body into submission, I find I can do more things that I hate, and do these hateful things faster and for a substantially longer time than when I started on the road to self-torture.

Recently, I've really begun to worry about my alleged sanity because I occasionally do something physical deliberately as an overt recreation. A couple of weeks back my 25-year-old son, John, and I climbed a mountain—a real, no-kidding 10,453-foot-high mountain—and we did it for fun!

John is disgustingly healthy and he goes to the gym because he loves it, but on this hike he was kind enough to at least breathe hard. I think he did that so I wouldn't feel bad for puffing like a steam loco- motive. I got to the top without major difficulty and I enjoyed both the hike and the time with my boy. As John ran down from the top, I wasn't able to go much faster than sort of a dedicated amble, but you can't have everything all at once.

In point of fact—and I'm admitting to a touch of pride in this— I can do more and there is materially less of me than I could and I was two years ago. It's a fact that I am getting older, but it is also a fact— at least in a few important ways—I'm also getting younger, which is confusing to everybody including me.

I like the idea I can actually keep up with my grandwidgets again. Also, while my dear bride the saintly Susan loves me pretty much without regard to my appearance—after all, even when age wasn't a factor nobody was going to call me pretty—I get a 19-year- old's kick out of the way she looks at my changing body now.

My dad, a very long time ago, told me, "When you get into a fight, if you can't have the whole meal at least get a biscuit." In my fight with the calendar, I'm by gosh going to get my biscuit.

● ● ● ●

30 Years. Can it be 30 years?

Everybody say it with me: "30 YEARS, 30 FREAKING YEARS!!!" Is that possible? I mean, can it be true? If the calendar is to be believed, and I have my doubts about any year that includes a leap day, I am on the teetering verge of marking 30 years as the lesser half of the couple Susan and Roger.

It was June 19, 1970 when the shy beauty with the enchanting brown eyes and the mane of chestnut hair changed her last name from Hubbard to Aylworth. Just why she made that choice has been open to public and private debate ever since. My darling, the saintly Susan, was not quite 18 when we first met. She was six months short of 20 when we married. I know her parents long wondered whatever possessed her to marry me, and frankly, I understand their reaction. It's an entirely reasonable question.

Why would this beautiful, intelligent, talented, angelic woman choose to hitch her wagon to my doubtful star? But hitch she did. She has followed me as I wandered from coast to coast. She has been the source, directly or otherwise, of all my important joys. She has stood by me through all my trials. In some mystical way it seems like we have been together all our lives, and at the same time it is beyond any rational possibility that 30 years have passed.

Together we have housebroken puppies and children, dealt with disease, disaster, and delight. We still giggle at each other over private jokes that we couldn't begin to explain to any other human being.

When we first met, Susan was a dazzling beauty with a crooked smile, and after 30 years of marriage she still takes my breath away. It wasn't all that long ago that our youngest, Rebecca, caught us kissing in the kitchen and announced, "Ooh! Get a room!"

There have been arguments, which means I said something stupid, defended it manfully, ultimately recognized what a jerk I had been, and begged for forgiveness. The only significant fault I can find with Susan is she is too modest, but beyond her modesty I am well and truly convinced my bride is perfect. (She will beat me for saying that, but I don't care.)

In 1970, looking up at a 30-year-high stack of life experiences would have been more than daunting. From this end, looking down, 30 years doesn't look like much more than a good start.

I still feel like I am on an extended date, and it is the best date of my entire life.

●　●　●　●

55 years in the making; now senior moments and menus

For five and a half decades I have tried to avoid it, but last Friday, without even so much as consulting me, it landed right on my graying head.

Friday—July 15 2005—was the 55th anniversary of my arrival on this troubled orb. I'm 55 years old, the double nickel, two fives! Just the concept of being that "freakin' old " is by itself daunting.

I am so old I remember back to when a "Beatle" was a bug. Yes, I know there is a difference in the spelling, but you get the point. I recall a time when my mother would never even consider leaving our modest San Francisco home without her hat and gloves. To my dad "casual Friday" would have meant slightly, ever so slightly, loosening the monochromatic tie around the highly starched collar of his white shirt.

I remember a time when if anybody started talking about "the war," they meant the big one, WWII. That rule applied to everybody but my Uncle Herbert, for whom "the war" could only mean World War I, where he served in the artillery in France.

I recall when the television was black and white, roughly the size of a walk-in closet, and, on a good day, included three whole channels. On those channels, good guys wore actual white hats, except for Adam Cartwright; Lucy got pregnant, although nobody really knew how; and Annette Funicello looked good, even wearing Mickey Mouse ears.

I remember drive-in movies, some of which I actually watched. I remember high school dances where I drenched myself in Jade East. (If you don't know what that is, ask your dad, or maybe your grandfather, or better yet, your mother.)

I recall with crystal clarity the day I met this dark-eyed beauty the first week of my freshman year in college, and, while I was enthralled by her waist-length mane of chestnut hair and her crooked smile, I promptly lost the phone number she gave me. It would be three months before we re-met and I began to fully appreciate how splendid the saintly Susan was and is.

I remember crummy jobs, sweltering apartments, cars that were held together by desperation and bailing wire, and an ever-growing collection of widgets who smiled so brightly they could make changing a diaper almost pleasurable.

As the years passed I was introduced to future brides, learned the joys associated with the title "grandpa," and said good-bye to my own parents. Now my two youngest widgets are on the teetering verge of the eternal adventure called marriage. For my part I can eat off the "senior" menu and fully justify a regular collection of "senior moments"— whoopee! I don't feel nearly as old as my calendar and mirror suggest I am, and when one of my grandwidgets is willing, I can roll on the floor and giggle right along with the rug rats.

Fifty-five years of living, also translates to 35 years with Susan, and of all the things I've ever done in my five and a half decades, falling in love with her and getting her to marry me are the easiest and smartest things I have ever done.

Yes, I am officially older than dirt, and while part of me would love to be an eternal teenager, there is no way I would give up or give back what my 55 years have brought me—though I wouldn't mind finding a new bottle of Jade East.

●　●　●　●

Advancing birthdays have positives

It happened again yesterday, and I really don't know what to do about it. For the 56th time in a row—in an unbroken string back to the middle of the last century, and without my specific permission—I suffered the indignity of yet another birthday.

Since I am not in the least prepared for the alternative, I can't really complain about having birthdays each year. Having said that, there is something increasingly disturbing about the steady, inexorable pace of good ol' Father Time as he marches to my genuinely final destination.

As much as I'd like to deny it, I'm beginning to suspect there is a high likelihood that I am in fact mortal. I'd like to predict that I will be cheerfully padding around this tortured globe well into the next century, but even my shaky grip on sanity tells me that ain't happening. It is that reality that makes my increasingly large collection of birthdays a bit daunting. At the same time, as the years stroll by, I continue to be enthralled with the parade.

Already this year, and the year is barely half over, my dear bride, the saintly Susan, and I have taken our first cruise and it was charming. We have also added a set of twin granddaughters and a lovely daughter-in-law to the clan so far this year.

My resident local granddaughter, Sydnie, has developed a heavenly inclination to see her grandpa get a full load of hugs anytime she comes to visit. Her older brother, Anthen, loves me to pieces and will be my friend forever as long as I let him play video games on my computer, and that's a trade I will happily accept. Caden, the baby of that branch of the clan, has recently demonstrated an inclination to giggle explosively when playing with me, which by itself goes a long way to make me feel younger.

I'm already getting excited about next year's edition of the family reunion—Aylapolooza II—when if all goes well, the entire clan will gather once again.

Beyond that I am thrilled by every minute I spend with Susan. With the household devoid of resident widgets and all of our children and grandchildren happy and healthy, my beloved and I can spend more time with each other, and not feel guilty for stealing time from some needy offspring. With nobody in the back seat chanting, "Are we there yet?" the two of us are actually contemplating some long road trips. We have discovered even driving across Nevada can be fun if we do it together.

We two are also continuing to spend time in the gym, and at some very practical level we are slowing and even reversing the aging process. It's all still good and there is so much left to do.

I have yet to write the great American novel, win a Pulitzer Prize, be named the sexiest man on the planet, or climb Mount Shasta, and I think I still have a shot at seeing the top of that mountain.

I have an untold number of yet-unborn grandwidgets to bounce on my knee and spoil shamelessly. Susan and I are already negotiating with the parents of our oldest grandwidgets to see if we can steal their kids for a week next year to take them on a trip and build some joyful memories of the "old folks."

Okay, I'm getting older, but there is so much left to do that older isn't all that bad an option after all.

Why the young have babies

Thunder would have been like whispering in church compared to the brain-homogenizing eruption of noise that exploded into my living room. Screams, shouts, squeals, and little voices that could etch glass with sound waves, crashed into the homestead like a tsunami, but the real chaos was yet to hit.

It was the evening of my birthday and my dear bride, the saintly Susan, and our daughter-in-law, Marie, were at a wedding reception. My birthday had been a joy beyond words. Susan and I got up late and then decided to go out for breakfast. We took an extended drive and explored some byways we have long been curious about.

Having an entirely unscheduled day to be with Susan ranks right near the absolute top of my happy list. Also near the top of that list is any time I can spend with the collection of small people who call me "Grandpa."

In recent weeks we have had the unusual pleasure of having Marie, our Matthew's dear wife, and their four smalls come down to have an extended visit with us and her parents, Mel and Sue, who live nearby.

The grandwidgets in their branch of the clan include Jacob, 4, and Elise, 2, along with a set of twins, Abby and Erin, three months old. Since I am pretty much worthless when it comes to breast-feeding infants and Erin and Abby are on a strictly-from-mommy diet, Susan and Marie took the twins with them to the wedding festivities that evening, leaving me with Jacob and Elise.

Frankly, I was stoked. These two little loves live in Oregon and I get to spend precious little time with them. I purchased boxes of animal crackers, a pair of small cars to drive on the floor, and even took the time to fold a couple of my world renowned paper airplanes, all with the intent of charming, fascinating and generally spoiling Jacob and Elise beyond any reasonable limits. They loved the cars, devoured the animal crackers, and were thrilled with the paper planes. I was a really big hit!

Then the doorbell rang.

My local son, Adam, along with his bride, Dana, and their little ones, Anthen, 8, Sydnie, 4, and Caden, 10 months old, had come by to wish me a happy natal day. When the little ones outside spotted the little ones inside, there was a flash of spontaneous mini-widget combustion. Jacob and Anthen ran screaming into each other's arms. Sydnie and Elise began shrieking with joy. While they were making more noise than a rock concert being conducted inside a boiler factory, it was a joyful sound. That's when Susan, Marie and the twins came home and the noise level rose still further.

The four larger smalls took over the spare bedroom where they were happily bounding from one bed to the other. Joy reigned supreme until Sydnie landed a little wrong in one of her leaps and managed to tear open a pre-existing blister on her cute little foot. Sydnie reacted with blood curdling screams. The three recently practiced parents of smalls responded with measured concern.

I had no idea what was wrong except my Sydnie was hurt. Her mom, Dana, scooped the frantic dolly into her arms. That's when I saw the blood. It was a matter of a few drops, but grandpa was already headed around the bend.

I wanted towels! I wanted somebody to boil water! I wanted a triage team! I was hurtling about the homestead, gathering bandages and issuing more orders to nobody in particular than the entire Joint Chiefs of Staff. Meanwhile quiet, patient Dana was taking care of business.

It was closing on bedtime for the smalls anyhow, so the still rational adults gathered up grandwidgets, put me in "time out" on the couch, and headed off to Adam's house.

Peace fell over Casa Aylworth III like a curtain.

It reminded me why Somebody with a lot more authority and brains than I has arranged the world so young people—not gray-headed grandpas with lots of birthdays—are the ones who have the babies.

● ● ● ●

Boys to (Little) Men

I may be letting something out of the bag, but I have a hunch most women already know it. Regardless of chronological age, most men are about 10 years old. Christmas is one time during the year when the allegedly adult male's inclination toward the juvenile blooms.

A man who would loudly proclaim his visceral hatred for shopping will romp through a toy store like a sugar-crazed 5-year-old on the excuse that he is just trying to find something for the kids. I can't speak for the other guys, but when I'm prowling through that toy store, I'm looking for things for me.

I love sling shots and model rockets, radio-controlled cars, building blocks, Erector sets, and anything that flies. BB-guns, little plastic army men, and model trains are exceedingly cool, and during Christmas I can wander through the toy store to my heart's delight, all under the cover of shopping for presents.

I've been particularly blessed because, with six sons, I not only could look wistfully at the pleasure machines of my youth, I could buy them and bring them home to some widget. If I was really lucky, the widget in question would rather play with the box, and let me play with the toy. Go to any park on Christmas afternoon and who is driving the RC car, who is flying the new plane, who is shooting hoops with the new ball? You got it: Dad!

The saintly Susan is of the opinion that I am stuck in an adolescent holding pattern. She has long known that males as a class, and most particularly her own dear hubby, are inclined to be children, and she accepts this aspect of my character with a certain restrained forbearance. That's good because I see no great danger of emotional maturity closing in on the horizon. I'm inclined to think we male types just want to play. The toys of our youth bring with them a small fraction of the youth itself.

It is hard to feel old and tired while sitting on the floor, surrounded by your own private army of tiny plastic soldiers, who will jump to your every command, conquer every evil foe, and never complain if you come back late from lunch. Bicycles, sleds, even computer games neither know nor care whether you made your sales quota for the month or outperformed your closest competitor, and as long as you are in charge, the good guys always win. (You even get to decide who the good guys are!)

In the past I've been able to share these experiences with a wonderful collection of bright-faced little boys, and one darling daughter, who thought they were playing with dad, when dad was really playing with them.

Now some of those little boys are becoming dads themselves, but wonder of wonders, they are providing me with new little boys, and even some little girls, to play with, and that's allowing me the excuse I need to buy kid toys through yet another generation. That's a good thing— maybe even necessary since, when it comes to Christmas and toys, I don't expect to grow up, or thankfully even grow old, any time soon.

● ● ● ●

Thanksgiving will include joy and tears

On my personal list of most favored holidays this coming Thursday ranks right near the top. Without most of the pressures associated with Christmas, Thanksgiving is a family day, a day to come together as a clan, to gather around a table happily burdened with the delicious food my dear bride, the saintly Susan, so lovingly prepares, and to be thankful for all good things.

From my perspective the good things are always easy to number: a glorious wife, who despite my laundry-list of failings, still loves me; seven of the greatest widgets on the planet, four truly fabulous daughters-in-law, nine grandwidgets, a house that shelters me, jobs that feed us, and the freedom to enjoy all of the above.

Traditionally, after an early afternoon Thanksgiving meal that borders on sublime gluttony, there has been a pick-up football game that has grown in popularity—and in the likelihood of major physical injury—as the widget Aylworths have grown to adulthood. Now with our children scattered truly from coast to coast, Susan and I will be heading two states east to join with a couple of our kids, Paul and Becca, who are both going to school back there, and most of Susan's family to mark Thanksgiving Day.

Even though most of the Aylworth family will be elsewhere, it will be a joyful event.

We will eat—I have a new recipe for a cheesecake I want to prepare—remember, laugh, and play. We may even convince some of the unwary or uniformed to join in one of our "nice, friendly" pickup football games.

I'll kid my darling daughter about the fact she is officially dating Mr. Wright. No, I'm not saying my baby has met "Mr. Right." I'm saying the young man she has been going out with lately is named Jonathan Wright.

We will pick on Paul about who he is or is not dating at the moment, celebrate the turkey and stuffing Susan's mother will prepare. She used to add giblets to her turkey dressing, but that came to an end 30-odd years ago when I asked what "the little black things" were. She's never been able to get over the "black things" image.

Besides the food and good cheer, we will also feel a twinge or two about those not present. One empty chair will be particularly felt this year, the high chair that would have been reserved for our grand-daughter, Allie Mae. Allie Mae was born in April and left us in July. There is a hole in all our hearts where "baby Allie" belongs.

I suspect tears will be shed at various Thanksgiving tables around the country where members of the clan Aylworth bow their heads in grateful prayer. We will shed tears over the loss and take joy in the blessing she was while she visited with us. We will also revel in the gifts that we have.

Regardless of the sorrows, I know as a given that I will greet every Thanksgiving with a lengthy list of blessings to count, and I know with equal certainty, the list will grow before the next Thanksgiving rolls around.

● ● ● ●

Christmas seasons more glorious than grand

Back in the days when there were more widgets in my house than available dollars, Christmas was done on a budget that would have made Tiny Tim wince.

Nowhere did that reality show more clearly than in the area of decorations. Window displays were made by little hands, using round-end scissors to cut out construction paper—and sometimes newsprint—trees, stars, angels and snowmen. Then, with the help of copious blobs of Elmer's glue, piles of glitter, amazing and jarring colors were randomly splattered over the cutouts that were then taped to the windows.

When we felt a little more financially flush, plain paper cutouts were used as stencils. We'd hold the star up to the window and then use spray can "snow" to make a reverse image. That ended when we discovered the spray snow could also be used to permanently etch glass. We had the ghostly image of Christmas trees and stars on those windows until the building was torn down.

When it came to Christmas trees, we often made our purchase just a couple of days before Christmas, when the selection—and the price—tended to be much smaller. The poor things were often specimens Charlie Brown would have passed over. The combination of available living room space and budget meant the trees were always small and often had to be mounted on a table so nobody would confuse them with a potted plant.

One, or rarely two, strands of the cheapest lights available were more than plenty for the midget tree.

We had a few precious heirloom ornaments that we got from our folks. They always had to be placed near the top of the tree, where they would be safe from the two- and four-legged marauders. Store-bought ornaments were cheap, plastic and usually ugly. I remember a collection of clear plastic icicles, suspended by what looked very much like bent paper clips. I recall feeling so grateful that I could buy the things for 11 cents each.

Hard-to-identify ornaments—crafted by small people, with more joy and enthusiasm than artistic skill—were the mainstay on the tree. Often these treasures included miniature pictures of the widget artists. While the artwork hasn't improved by aging, the pictures of the little people who once gathered around those trees makes them increasingly precious.

Candy canes festooned the tree from top to bottom. The canes on the bottom branches had a curious habit of disappearing. When our senior son, Aaron, was about 3, he explained the vanishing candy. An invisible lion lived under the table that held the tree and in the "dark time" the lion would creep out and snatch canes. I'm sure it was true because there was always a stack of candy cane wrappers under the table where the invisible lion had left them.

There were Christmases that were so economically lean that friends and people from church made our family the "project." I both want to smile and cry when I think about a season many years ago when I was out of work, and Susan and our then two sons, Aaron and Adam, were recovering from injuries suffered in a terrible traffic accident. Gifts and boxes of food appeared on our front porch like Santa himself had made the deliveries.

This year things are different. Most of the widgets are spread to the four winds and even the two families that live locally will be spending at least part of Christmas with others. Finances will be easier and the decorations substantially grander, but there will be no less joy around the tree.

While we often were aware we didn't have any money, we never felt "poor." We always had a roof over our heads, enough to eat, and we had love. That made it a joyful holiday for all of us.

● ● ● ●

Christmas will be quieter this year

Today, Christmas day, will be quieter in Casa Aylworth this year than it has been in many decades past. For the first time since 1972 our household will not include one resident widget.

In the past year we married off our two youngest, and John, our lone remaining unattached offspring, lives in the home he bought last April. The net result is my dear bride, the saintly Susan, and I will greet Christmas morning without a herd of children waiting to thunder down the hall to begin plundering the presents.

Our kids created their own tradition on this point. Every

Christmas Eve all of the resident smalls would spend the night in a single bedroom. When that meant seven were crammed into the room, it made for a decidedly cozy night. They packed in mattresses and sleeping bags and talked and giggled for most of the night.

House rules required that no widget enter the living room on Christmas morning until a parent was present. That meant that some time shortly after dawn, a collection of soprano voices started singing carols, giggling, and making noises just loud enough to awaken a parental unit without making anybody angry.

Once the mob was set free, they would descend on a tree piled high with beautifully wrapped presents. Like a swarm of two-legged locusts these little sweeties would rampage through their gifts and in about 30 minutes the living room was two feet deep in shredded wrapping paper. Then they ran to the kitchen to devour the hot homemade sweet rolls Mom was pulling from the oven.

Christmas Eves have always been particularly important in my crowd.

Susan, who is a dynamic cook, turns her talents to a huge pot of humble—usually lentil—soup. To this she adds a big plate of home-made rolls. By the light of the Christmas tree, augmented by a flash-light if necessary, we sit around and read the old story of the poor carpenter and his espoused wife. We talk about the little town, crowded by people who had come to pay their taxes, and the fact there was no room at the inn. With a battered and bedraggled nativity scene as a visual aid, we tell our little ones about the babe, born in a stable, and laid in a manger.

For many years the Casa Aylworth included a big red barn that was periodically inhabited by cows, horses, chickens and turkeys, even a few goats. The resident widgets had a sense of what a night in a stable was like, and they understood stables, and mangers, and tiny babies.

This year our babies will be with other people they love. They are creating their own family traditions.

As I often do, I'll be working this Christmas, but before I go to the newsroom, Susan and I will sit before our own small tree and share gifts. We will have slept a little later and the post-present-opening debris will be much less.

I know we will miss our little ones, but I also know how blessed this Christmas will be. We will see our kids and grandkids. It's not like we are being abandoned, but this morning will be for us, a couple. Susan, my best friend in the world, and I will share time, memories, gifts and love.

Merry Christmas to all.

● ● ● ●

A Christmas wish: Some bright ideas for presents

With Thanksgiving rapidly disappearing into the rearview mirror, I find myself careening toward one of the most treacherous seasons of the year. It's Christmas present buying time. Be afraid, be very afraid!

In point of fact, buying presents *per se* doesn't scare me. I genuinely adore buying gifts for the people I love. I suspect that at some deep psychological level I'm trying to win their affection with retail therapy, but whatever my internal motivation, I enjoy getting things for the dear people in my corner of the cosmos.

I can also be really good at gift giving. If I'm buying for my six sons, my grandsons, or my lone son-in-law, I'm a pro! I just wander around the store until I see something I want to play with, then I buy it for the kid in question. It is an approach I understand based on 57 1/2 years of being on the boy side of the gene pool.

It is on the other side of that pool where the problems exist. With girls under about the age of 8, I have a fighting chance to make a successful gift selection. At that point in their maturation the relative distinction between male and female tastes in presents is pretty small.

Boys and girls both like to play with dolls at that point. The only difference is boy dolls are called action figures. I also know I can pretty much be sure of scoring good grandpa points with rocking horses, tricycles, drawing supplies or building blocks.

Then somewhere in those upper single-digit years the great divide between the sexes begins to take place. Sometimes the genetic division asserts itself earlier. My adorable 6-year-old granddaughter Sydnie is still in the age range where I have some hope of predicting her wants and wishes, but she is already providing hints that things are about to change. This blonde dolly with the high-intensity smile already views shoe shopping as a significant recreational activity. I fear she runs the clear risk of being a "teenager" by the time she turns 8.

It is when I am trying to pick gifts for the females in my life—those who have hit their teens or older—that the challenges occur. I confess despite decades of sincerely trying, I don't begin to understand the thinking process of the female of the species, and that includes my dear bride, the saintly Susan.

What's more when I prod her into providing me a Christmas list, she comes up with things like a slotted spoon, wool socks and a new pencil sharpener.

To complicate matters even further, her birthday is Dec. 21. Not only do I need to select something for the biggest holiday of the calendar, but I need to be brilliant four days prior to Santa's arrival, and then remember not to wrap the birthday gift in Christmas paper.

Occasionally I do get it right.

Some years back I arranged to have a diamond ring, that Susan had never been able to wear, resized to fit her. I didn't think it was such a big deal—the ring was already hers, after all. When she opened the box, she gasped, began to sob and gave me a big wet kiss.

Last year for her birthday I gave her an electronic drum set. Susan was an all-state drummer in her high school days back in Arizona, and I suspected she would love to pick up her sticks again. I was right then, too.

Then there is this year. I have no clues, no guesses, and so far no hints. I haven't even been asked to buy another slotted spoon, but I'm not giving up. Little gasps, happy tears, and big wet kisses still rank as high motivation for me to get the gift right.

● ● ● ●

Calendar playing a trick: 1968 wasn't 40 years ago

Since we are nearly two months into it, I figured it wouldn't come as too much of a shock if I told you that it is the year 2008. To look at 2008, it doesn't appear to be all that exciting. Oh sure, it is both a leap year and a presidential election year, but those two things happen quadrennially whether we want them to or not.

It also isn't one of those mystical years that ends in one or more zeroes, which seem to force people to look forward with fear and trembling, or backward with longing. Having said all that, this is the year that recently got my attention.

I was watching the History Channel on television—my widgets claim that if the end of the world happens and it is not announced on the History Channel, I'll miss it entirely—when a show came on about 1968. For a bunch of reasons, 1968 was a significant year for me, so I was immediately fascinated. It was while sitting there in the happy confines of Casa Aylworth III, it suddenly hit me that 1968 was 40 years ago. Let me say that slowly: 40 whole, entire, incredible years ago. That is a pile of decades that is almost impossible to comprehend.

For me that 40 years ago was yesterday, and it was a yesterday that in many ways shaped my life and my world view.

In February 1968 I was in the last semester of my senior year at Abraham Lincoln High in San Francisco. At the time my biggest challenge in life was how to fund my senior prom. The Haight-Ashbury neighborhood was about a mile and a half from my house. Flower Power was in full bloom. I may well have been the only person in my graduating class who made it through that year without ever getting stoned.

Pot never interested me and, except for an unfortunate incident with a large bottle of Vicks Formula 44 cough medicine, I never got drunk, either. For my part I genuinely found life intoxicating without chemical enhancement.

However, while my life tended to be safe and happy—in point of fact I was miserable a significant portion of the time, but it was the sort of undifferentiated misery experienced by all adolescent males regardless of justification—the world I lived in was in turmoil.

Before the year ended there were two world-changing assassinations, riots raged and razed across the nations, peace marches that were anything but peaceful shook towns and school campuses from coast to coast, a presidential nominating convention turned into a war zone, and a whole generation learned the phrase "Tet offensive."

In my high school, which on a day-to-day basis often defined the outlines of my world, an arsonist hit campus, a race riot erupted during lunch, and the drama teacher cast a black football player as a white Southern aristocrat in the play, "Little Foxes," because he was the right person for the role.

We had a student walkout and a teachers' strike. It was the year I was infected with the news bug, and it was the first year I ever carried a press card. I was a reporter for the "Lincoln Log."

In April I was accepted at the university of my choice, and in June I graduated from high school, with the sure knowledge that I was in no way prepared to make a living in the big world. It was the summer I had my first full-time job as an amazingly inept painter's helper working in the California Academy of Sciences in Golden Gate Park.

It was during student orientation, in my first week at college, that I met the entrancing beauty with the crooked smile from nowhere Arizona who would become my life's companion.

It was a strident, violent, bloody, frightening, peaceful, warm, loving and beautiful year, and it was yesterday, and today, and 40 years ago.

There are scenes, snatches, moments, images of 1968, that will always live within me. There are names, places, moments, experiences I will never forget, and in a very real sense, 1968 will always be part of my NOW, no matter how long ago it was.

● ● ● ●

Awakening to a
mindless present

Awakening to a mindless present

I woke up this morning and discovered my brain is empty. I've been running on fumes for a long time, so it shouldn't have really come as much of a shock, but I'm still not thrilled with the situation.

The problem is, I don't have any really good ways to jump-start an empty head. It struck me that something akin to a mental battery charger would be really handy at a moment like this. I could connect a couple of alligator clips to my ears, set the machine to trickle charge, then sit in the corner for four or five hours while I reload the cerebral void.

Unfortunately the only real way I know to fill the brain is the laborious effort of thinking. Thinking has its place, but it is not something you want to do in public. Let somebody catch you in the middle of a deep ponder and all of a sudden you get a reputation. You are branded a nerd.

Around my house I have trouble enough of that sort. As a matter of entertainment choice, I prefer to watch the History Channel over MTV and that immediately has my household widgets up in arms. Since we first got a satellite dish, my kids have maintained television should consist of drooler half-hour sit-coms, or music videos. Since my brain drain, I can think of no good reason to disagree with them.

I suspect my sudden collapse of brain matter may in fact have positive side effects. For one thing, I will be able to watch network television without taking sedatives.

At the other end of the mental agenda, I always rather enjoyed having a brain. There was a certain pleasure associated with being brighter than a banana slug. I liked it when friends and colleagues asked me questions and expected rational, and sometimes even insightful responses. I liked being able to read books with words longer than four letters and understanding their meanings.

It amused me to be able to think through a problem and find a solution.

Now I'm relegated to calling the psychic hotline or the television tarot lady, and reading the daily horoscope to plan my life. Of course there is always the great philosophical observation, "I think, therefore I am."

Does that mean that now I am not? If I had an answer to that I might still claim to have a brain, which would be another conundrum. If I were smart enough, I wouldn't let this intellectual decline bother me. After all, there are scores of American politicians who never had a brain in the first place and it never seemed to hurt their careers one whit.

● ● ● ●

Federal document expands my capacity to boggle

After five-plus decades wandering around this humble orb, I sometimes think my capacity to be astounded has reached full, but then something comes along to prove beyond a doubt the world can be stranger than I had already anticipated.

I attained a new level of boggle not long ago when I decided to do something that by itself is not exactly sane.

To celebrate, or at least recognize, my recently passed birthday, I decided to take another shot at climbing Mount Shasta, a near 15,000-foot high volcano at the north end of the Sacramento Valley.

The hike itself was an exercise in insanity, but before I set foot on the mountain I ran into something much more frightening than an old fat grandfather trying to climb a volcano—the federal government.

Every year, about 15,000 would-be mountain climbers make more or less successful efforts to struggle up the steep sides of Shasta.

The climbers encounter steep slopes, elevations where oxygen isn't much more than a memory, loose rock and ash slopes that are not unlike trying to hike up a near vertical beach, and blindingly white snow fields where the combination of altitude and summer sun can blister exposed skin in less time than it takes to tell, but there is one thing they won't find—restrooms.

There are the ever popular pit-toilets at Bunny Flats, where would-be climbers park. From there to the windswept, snow-clad summit, the only official place to unburden one's colon is a set of "solar, composting toilets," at Horse Camp, about an hour's hike in from the parking lot.

I frankly have no clue what a solar composting toilet is, and whatever they are, they open only on even numbered days. Beyond these genuinely modest facilities, Mount Shasta is officially a poop-free zone.

Humans are prohibited from leaving anything on the mountain and that "anything" is a truly all inclusive word.

That brings us to what in the parlance of federal regulations is "CFR 261.11d," the "human waste packout system."

In simple terms the rule is, "You poop it, you scoop it!"

After registering as a would-be Shasta climber at the National Forest office, I was provided a human poop disposal kit that comes with a plastic bag, a couple of paper bags with kitty litter in them and a sheet of instructions.

It was this sheet of instructions that renewed my faith in my capacity to boggle.

On one side of the 10.5 by 17 inch sheet of paper there are distressingly detailed directions on how to "eliminate such problems"— and you know somebody giggled like mad as he or she wrote that little play on words. However, it was the reverse side of the directions that prompted my boggle.

Flip the directions over and you have an official, federally approved, poop target.

The backside of the sheet has a bull's eye printed in the center and the expanding rings are numbered from 10 in the dead center to 5 on the outer edge. I know life is competitive, but this is a contest I had never contemplated.

I suppose there is a certain warm feeling to be had in doing any project well, but if I used the target—and I most certainly did not!—who records my score? Is there a prize for accurate . . . ah . . . er . . . well . . . pooping? If my aim proves less than perfect, is there a penalty? Do I have to pass a qualifying heat before I earn the right to compete with the big boys?

In my case, the poop target has attained the status of a souvenir, so I guess I'm officially out of the competition anyhow, which is probably a good thing, because I have no idea where I would display a winning entry.

●　●　●　●

Bags of goo taking over kitchen

Imagine this scenario: You're walking through the mall, juggling your kids and your newly acquired possessions, when a strange man, carrying a shopping bag and looking slightly frantic, runs up to you. He says, "Hi, my name is Roger. Would you like a bag of goo?"

I suspect that approach would earn me some really impressive slaps in the face, but I've got to figure something out before the stuff entirely takes over my kitchen.

The goo began as an officially friendly gesture. About a month ago, Alan, a coworker who is truly a prince of a gentleman—his only apparent failing is he roots for the Philadelphia Eagles—offered to give me a recipe for "Amish Friendship Bread."

Without giving it much thought, I said sure. A few days later

Alan showed up with a photocopied recipe and a gallon-sized plastic bag partially filled with off-white goo. For the most part the recipe was a list of instructions for the goo's care and feeding.

Under no circumstances was I to refrigerate the mess. I was to keep it either in the bag or a crockery bowl, and on a tight schedule I was—depending on the day—to mash the bag or feed it a combination of sugar, milk and flour.

Before sending me home with the mess, Alan warned me to be careful when I open the bag because the smell can be overpowering. I've done a lot of baking in recent years, but I never before found myself having to sneak up on any of the ingredients. Then again I never had a recipe that included a growing mass of goo.

I took the stuff home and religiously followed the instructions, mashing or mixing as directed, and I quickly recognized two facts: First, the mixture produced an awful lot of gas, and secondly it was growing—a lot.

On day 10 of the process, per instructions, I made up a batch of the bread and divided the remaining goo into four other gallon bags, three of which I was supposed to pass on to some other unsuspecting soul.

The bread turned out to be really good, but I soon discovered that trying to hand out bags of goo is about as easy as giving away puppies—and puppies are a lot cuter. On top of that the growing number of bags in the corner of the kitchen counter all require feeding and mashing and the entire group continues to grow and gas with cheerful microbial abandon.

My dear bride, the saintly Susan, knowing that the goo was beginning to make me babble, tried to get a friend to take a bag full.

"Oh gee! No thanks," said the friend. "Maybe you can give this stuff to somebody who is a real dunce. Oops, I mean to some good person who has never seen it before," she suggested. Uh-huh.

I've got to figure out what to do with this stuff. Maybe I can get somebody to do a remake of the movie "The Blob." This stuff would make a great prop. It doesn't eat human flesh, at least not as far as I know, and at the end of the filming it makes bread that tastes better than most space aliens, at least the ones I've tasted.

On the other hand, I could follow Steve McQueen's lead. As I remember he did in the original Blob by freezing it when it oozed into a theater.

Maybe that's why the first instruction on the recipe sheet is, "Don't Refrigerate." Now that's a thought. . . . But then, what would I do with a lot of dead goo?

I'm still working on a solution, but don't be surprised if, next time you're in the mall, a frantic-looking man runs up to you and asks, "Would like a bag of goo?

● ● ● ●

It's difficult to become the curmudgeon of my dreams

I've gone through life trying to sell a certain image to the world. I'd like to fancy myself a tough, no-nonsense, hard-boiled, cynical newspaper reporter.

This person has a Clark Gable stare, two-day's growth of beard, and wears a brimmed hat with a press card in the band. His tie is askew, and his shirt sleeves are rolled above the elbow. He breakfasts on cold chili beans and warm root beer. He snarls, complains about everything, and can scare a tree if he tries.

It is a persona I have consistently tried to nurture, and apparently I have been a total flop at it. Oh, I can be as outraged as anybody when I see the inhumane things that humans do to each other. Governmental arrogance or stupidity, or worse still arrogant stupidity, can make me apoplectic.

I've been able to growl—even snarl—at the occasional bureaucrat with an imperious manner and more rules than brains, but the fact of the matter is I don't have it in me to be the hard-edged curmudgeon of my dreams.

I smile at small children, try to be courteous to just about everybody, and feel like the scum of the earth when I lose my temper—even when the target of my outrage truly deserved the verbal thumping.

I think kittens are cute, will play with puppies, and enjoy bouncing babies—particularly my own grandwidgets—on my knee. I've been known to raise my voice in the office, but it is usually to find out who swiped my doughnut.

I suppose there may be a handful of people in the world who think I am truly a hard person, but they aren't people who know me well or can pronounce my last name. (If beer is worth a dime, how much is Ayl-worth?)

For most of the world, I am as transparent as glass.

A woman who once worked for me watched my I'm-a-hard-old-newspaper-guy act for about three days. On the fourth day I walked into my office to find a stuffed Winnie the Pooh bear sitting on my desk, with a note that read, "You are about as scary as this bear."

I still keep Winnie on my desk.

I have been known to rampage around like a bull elephant with a cactus up his nose, if somebody challenges my honesty, does anything negative toward my kids, or looks cross-eyed at the saintly Susan. I can also sit at my desk and sob as I write a story about a child who died needlessly, about a tragedy that could have been avoided, or about a life that was wasted.

At the same time I can get teary about a hero who tries to avoid recognition, a person or group who does good because it is right, not because they will get an inch of print, and about the simple, honest act of being human.

No, I'll never sell the tough guy image. Tough guys don't cry over their computer keyboards, but if I was all that tough, I don't think I'd be somebody I'd want to know.

● ● ● ●

Dreadlocks and other lessons to re-learn

I like to think of myself as a wonderfully open-minded soul who treats the world—except gophers—with undiluted kindness and equanimity. I also like to think of myself as tall, handsome, and intelligent, so it comes as no great surprise that my vision of myself and reality don't always jive.

That point smacked me firmly in the face a bit ago.

I wandered into one of those establishments that are laughingly referred to as "convenience stores" to buy a soda. In front of me in line was an enormous young man. His hair was bundled into a pony-tail of unruly dreadlocks. Massive calves bulged out of knee-length shorts. To say this guy was big is just way short of the mark. He could throw enough shade to darken the sky in two or three zip codes all at once.

As far as I was concerned everything about this fellow radiated menace. I was pretty sure if I met him in a dark alley, I would die of terror before he so much as scowled at me. On top of all this, too many years reporting on cops and robbers has endowed me with a certain penchant for paranoia.

This particular variety of commercial establishment is sometimes referred to as a "stop and rob" by police, and I was more than mildly concerned about the potential for criminality happening right before my aging, blood-shot eyes.

In front of this mountain with feet was a little boy—maybe 10. The boy, like most kids his age, reminded me of one of my own grandwidgets. It was well into the middle afternoon, and long past the lunch rush, but the little guy was hungry and he wanted a hot dog. There was one lone hot dog, rather pathetically turning on the cooking rollers in the back of the heating cabinet. Eagerly the little boy paid for it.

Then, with some difficulty—using a pair of tongs—he managed to snag the lonely wiener, but before the lad could do something with his would-be lunch the tube-steak escaped the tongs and tumbled onto the much less than hygienic floor. The boy was trying to scrape the visible dirt off the dog, and was clearly more embarrassed by his own perceived clumsiness than about any additional flavoring the floor might have added to his lunch.

What got my attention was the dreadlock-adorned "menace" in front of me who was clearly both touched and concerned about the little boy's plight.

"Ah, bro! That's just wrong. Tell the guy. He will get you your money back," said the young mountain, in a gentle and startlingly high-pitched voice. The dreadlocked young man was trying to help the little stranger and he was being gentle, warm, and sincerely supportive.

As I watched the interplay and heard the words, my image of the guy in front of me changed dramatically. He was obviously a good guy, somebody I would like to know, a man I would be honored to call friend, and I felt like the bottom two inches of sludge in a septic tank.

Nobody likes to face hard proof he is a jerk, but there it was. With nothing more to go on than appearance, I had decided this man was scary, and perhaps worse still, a potential criminal. Then he proved he was a gentleman and a gentle man, and I was dumb as a door knob.

I learned something that day. It was something I already knew, but I clearly needed to re-learn it. Maybe I ought to find out how I'd look in dreadlocks. That could be a learning experience, too.

Mysteries that tease us all

There are mysteries in the world that will forever tease the mind of the human animal.

These are questions of such grandeur and momentous import that their true answers are almost certainly beyond the comprehension of mere mortals.

These are the questions that try our souls and are the refiners fire of intellectual steel.

Who, for example, would return an ice cream box to the freezer with one teaspoon of ice cream remaining?

Why is it, if your car ever breaks down, it will happen the day before you planned to leave on your vacation?

Why is it the hottest day of the year falls always on a workday?

Conversely, why does the coldest, wettest day of the year happen on a weekend?

How do small children know the exact spot on the precise step to leave the toy to make sure you achieve two and a half flips in a pike position before crashing at the bottom of the stairs?

Why is it that men who can sleep comfortably naked in a blizzard marry women who think 113-degrees is a perfectly reasonable room temperature for slumber?

Explain why, no matter how wide the tie it never covers the stain on your shirt?

How is it the one time in 14 years you suffer a brain cramp and blow through a stop sign is also the day you have a highway patrolman behind you?

Why do pipes rupture and sinks leak only after all the stores are closed, and the plumbers are on double time and a half?

Why does the toilet paper always run out when you're the one in the bathroom?

Who tells everybody else when you are going to the grocery store so they all can get in line five seconds before you?

Why is it, when a crazy person calls your office, you're the one to answer the phone?

How can a woman with the body of a goddess eat like a horse and never gain a pound, and the guy who looks like a horse can gain weight on a diet that would starve a gerbil?

Why is the shortest distance between two points always some place where the roads don't go?

Why is the person you most thoroughly despised in high school the only one you can recognize at the reunion?

Why does a man's wisdom only arrive when his youth has departed?

How can a kid easily stick his head into a place he can't possibly pull his head out of?

How do telephone solicitors always know when you just sat down to dinner?

How can television producers all come up with the same stupid plot for a sit-com and still believe they have ever had an original idea?

Why do all small appliances outlive their warranty by 11.3 seconds?

Why is it on the day the alien mother-ship lands in your front yard you have no film for the camera?

How come if you do it, whatever the "it" is, 999 times perfectly, nobody is around, but do it once badly and you can guarantee you'll have an audience?

Why is it that parts that come off the car so easily are almost impossible to get back on?

How do buttons know to come off at just the second that will make you look most foolish?

Why isn't stupidity painful?

Why would anybody think chopped goose liver is a food?

How can a woman as intelligent, articulate, and breathtaking as the saintly Susan fall in love with me?

These are the questions that taunt us. They may never be answered, but sometimes the last thing we could ever want is an answer.

● ● ● ●

For the most part, clothes improve the view

If you take one look at me, it is easy to figure out what led me to the conclusion that most people on the planet look materially better with their clothes on. While there may in fact be a handful of exceptions, I am convinced nakedness is a tactical error and a major fashion faux pas for the vast majority of the population.

I'll be the first to admit, I certainly fit into the naked-is-nasty class of human forms. I make a serious effort to avoid seeing myself in the buff. Heck, I'd shower with my clothes on if I could figure out a good way to do it.

Thankfully, given the weather and local customs, there is very little chance of me having to deal with a naked person strolling down the street. However, there is one part of my public world where nudity does happen.

Several years back I joined a health club, and over a long slow stretch I have begun to beat my pitiful form into some level of fitness. Since I usually hit the gym after work, I have to change in the locker room.

Going back to my days in junior high school, I have never been what you would call a big fan of locker rooms. A roomful of sweaty, hairy, unclad males, ranks right up there with train wrecks and city dumps among things I try to avoid. Combine that view with the . . . ah . . . well fragrance of even the most hygienic locker room, and you have a mix that would offend a nearsighted goat with a head cold.

Since I am less than impressed with my appearance—dressed or otherwise—I make a genuine effort not to inflict my naked visage on some unsuspecting soul. With that goal in mind, I arrange my gym clothes in a carefully thought out order before I take off so much as my tie. From the instant my first button is unfastened, I can be fully dressed in my workout duds in about 90 seconds. Then I beat feet the heck out of the locker room in search of something similar to fresh air.

One of the things I have discovered, to my dismay, is my disinclination to be seen in the buff is not a universal constant. I can't speak to the female half of the world—since I have never spent any time in a women's locker room—but there is a segment of the guy side of the population that seems not the least bit affected by, or even particularly aware they are naked. They wander around with a towel over their shoulder, apparently unconcerned, and certainly uninhibited by their lack of attire.

I've also observed that there is absolutely no connection between the perfection of the male form, and the inclination to parade that form around.

My son John, who, until he took a job 100 miles away, used to share a gym with me, has the body of a young Greek god, and if anything, he is more modest than I am when it comes to nude strolling. He once observed that among some people there is a culture of "casual naked," and I have to agree, although I may not join that parade.

I suppose there is something to be said for being at ease in one's body. I mean I do rather like me, even if I am about as aesthetically pleasing as a walrus in a tu-tu. Having said that, within some obvious limitations, people have a right to strut their . . . well . . . er . . . ah . . . stuff, even if that stuff is naked. Even though I kind of wish they wouldn't.

●　●　●　●

'Rhonda' makes visit to my wallet

There are a few things in life that I consider absolute rules. The sun comes up in the east. Gravity works. Taxes are eternal, not internal, and anything that tastes good is not on the diet.

On that same list of rules is the expectation that my bank only gives out my money when I say so, but that's a rule I may have to reconsider.

My faith in that rule was shaken by a woman who I am absolutely certain isn't Rhonda Watkins. I know this person isn't Rhonda, because that's who she says she is.

Recently my dear bride, the saintly Susan, was updating the family financial records by way of our bank's Internet site. That's when she discovered an $80 and change check she couldn't identify.

Knowing that her loving hubby has a talent for writing out-of-sequence checks and failing to record them in the book, she called me at work to ask about the surprise item.

I had absolutely no memory of the check, but that is no great shock because I get lost driving home about three times a month. Susan got a digital image of the check online and that's when we were introduced to Rhonda.

To our substantial consternation, the check showed Rhonda's name printed right above mine, along with an address in Sacramento, a phone number, and a pair of utterly bogus driver's license numbers.

Dear sweet Rhonda was passing checks that were as phony as the license numbers and dipping aggressively into our always anemic bank account. In short order Susan determined our new friend had sucked about $850 out of our finances.

For a lot of folks, or so I'm told, $850 is nothing much more than pocket change, but my pockets are much shallower than that, and these unplanned withdrawals looked very much like the national debt to Susan and me.

Susan immediately got on the phone to the bank to get this nonsense brought to a screaming halt, but there is more than one kind of nonsense in the world.

As Susan explained about Rhonda, our "helpful" banker seemed to think a wife finding her hubby's and another woman's name on a check was more an issue for marriage counseling than fraud investigation. Using little words, so the banker could understand, Susan made it clear Rhonda wasn't part of our lives or accounts and she thought, just maybe, the bank shouldn't be accepting checks from random people off the street.

I think the short words got through because all of a sudden the banker was willing to talk, and he said he would send us a collection of forms to file. Meanwhile Rhonda was still treating our checkbook like her personal piggy bank.

That's when we met Nick. Nick is a real, breathing person who works at our neighborhood bank branch. He was immediately outraged that somebody would be stealing from an account in his bank. He apologized for any hint that Rhonda and I might be more than strangers, and proceeded to close down accounts, open new ones, and bounce money around to make it all work.

Now about getting our $850 back—well, that was going to take a little longer, because he couldn't just do it. The magical denizens of the mysterious "fraud investigations office" had to waive their wands to make that happen, and they are by nature a suspicious lot.

So we found ourselves meeting with a nice police officer, filling out more forms, swearing that we aren't crooks, and guaranteeing after nearly 30 years of banking with this institution that we hadn't suddenly chosen to dive into the realm of larceny.

Just how Rhonda got the necessary names and numbers to plunder our paltry finances remains a mystery to me, but we are going to do what little we can to make sure she keeps her sticky fingers to herself in the future.

We purchased a document shredder and are turning anything that remotely resembles financial records into confetti. We have new checks, new ATM cards, and significant desire to kick Rhonda right in her . . . checkbook.

● ● ● ●

Stepping back from the dark side: Confession of a faker baker

After years of subterfuge and deception, I have a confession to make. I am a baking fraud. It is a sad thing to admit, but truth is truth and it is time to come clean. I have been living a serious Betty Crocker, Pillsbury Doughboy lie. It's time I said it. "Hi, I'm Roger, and—oh this is so hard—I'm a faker baker."

As things tend to do, my problem began with good intentions. I would take the hours required to lovingly blend brown and white sugar, flour, butter, spices, heavy cream, real vanilla, chopped nuts, chocolate chips, butterscotch, raisins and a host of other heavenly ingredients, to create glorious and masterful works of the baker's art. I made chocolate chip and oatmeal cookies, ginger bread, brownies by the pile, cakes, lemon meringue pies, and I thing I call "seven-layer goodie" that is more addictive that heroin.

I made them from scratch. I'd bring my baked goods to work. I'd share them with friends. I'd take them to all sorts of church functions, and I would bask in the warm light of praise and amazement at my culinary glory. It got so people began to expect me to have the goods for them. Performance pressure mounted endlessly.

It was in the face of this pressure that my dedication to Epicurean purity cracked.

At first it was little things. I started using frozen pie crusts. When nobody seemed to notice, I was tempted to step further into the dark side. The next thing I knew I was buying pre-mixed chocolate chip cookie dough.

It was so easy. I'd hide the tubes of dough in my shopping cart. Then in the privacy of my own kitchen, after closing all of the blinds, I could cut chunks of dough onto the cookie sheets, without ever mixing a single ingredient. People loved what the Pillsbury Doughboy fixed up for me. I found if I left the cookies in a hot car before delivering them, I could even create the impression they had just come out of the oven. I was losing my soul!

There followed an endless array of boxes, mixes, and already prepared goodies. I tried to assuage my guilt by saying I was still doing the cooking. It was, after all, up to me to see they didn't burn. Yet I couldn't get away from the fact that a mentally challenged monkey, lacking in opposable thumbs, could do what I was doing.

I hadn't reached the point where I would go into a store, buy a bag of Oreos, put them on a paper plate and claim I had just baked them, but it was coming. I could see the day when I would hand out Pop-Tarts, still in the package, and try to claim I had made them myself. My future was bleak.

Then I met this good man, an honorable man, a man named Joseph, who had both unreasonable faith in me, and a serious addiction to oatmeal-raisin cookies. As far as I can tell, and if I'm wrong please don't correct me, nobody makes prefab oatmeal-raisin cookies.

I was forced to go back to my roots, to once again use a recipe and a mixing bowl. It was hard, but it felt good! Now, I'm on the road to recovery. I have faith that with the support of my dear bride, the saintly Susan, and Joseph's endless appetite for oatmeal and raisins, I can step back into the light, open the curtains in my kitchen, and scorn the temptations of that wretched Doughboy.

Reclaim my youth? Why? Is it missing?

Not long ago my dear bride, the saintly Susan, and I rented a silly comedy film centered on four middle-aged guys who take off on a cross-country motorcycle tour. The road trip is sort of vehicular therapy for the graying quartet, and each is trying to claim some fragment of his fading youth.

It was one of those films so predictable you are embarrassed to laugh at the inane gags, but you laugh despite yourself. As we switched off the DVR, my bride asked, "What would you do to reclaim your youth?"

I was a little stunned at the question. My first thought was, "Reclaim my youth? Why, is it missing?"

I didn't misplace my youth. I used it! Here and there it might be fairly observed that I misspent some portions of it. Beyond that I haven't surrendered it. There are youthful, even child-like, things I still revel in.

I adore the vision of a starry night. The sound of thunder still makes me tingle. I love the screeching call of a hawk circling high overhead. I love to walk, and occasionally run. I love to body surf in the cold Pacific. While I've never been all that good with my hands, I love to start and successfully finish a project around the house.

Even though I am about as graceful as a three-legged buffalo, I enjoy dancing—ballroom or rock. I also have never gotten past my love of 60s rock music.

Few things in the world are more fun for me than riding around in the wonderful pickup my wife gave me as a birthday present, while singing along with some good song on the radio's oldies station.

The ongoing battle with my waistline makes such glorious gluttony rare, but I love a good greasy, artery-clogging bacon cheeseburger.

I remain a dedicated 49ers fan, and I exult in their successes, which means in recent years I haven't been all that exultant.

Most days—about seven out of 10—I enjoy what I do for a living. I love the daily battle with deadlines. It still feels great to come up with a genuine "scoop," although nobody has said the word scoop in 30 years. The opportunity to meet and talk to interesting, involved, achieving people has never lost a bit of its charm for me. It is the case I'm no longer as eager as I once was to rush to the sound of the sirens. I've seen more than my full fair share of tragedy, but at the same time I still am profoundly impressed by the courage, dedication, intelligence and compassion of the men and women in uniform who do respond to these scenes.

I adore playing with babies, especially my grandwidgets. From Austin (who is now driving!) to the youngest—Becca's firstborn, Caleb, and Adam's red-haired Dallin—they are all fun people, more precious than gold.

I like a brilliant shine on my shoes, a crisply ironed shirt, and a pair of torn and patched jeans that not even a mother could love.

Chronologically, I am several years beyond what most calendars would call middle-aged, but to my knowledge I have never had a mid-life crisis. I can't imagine what I would do with one. I have no desire to own or drive a red sports car. The thought of cavorting with some twenty-something female, no matter how comely, is abhorrent to me for a whole range of reasons. Just the concept of being "involved" with a woman younger than most of my kids, is enough to make me shudder. Beyond that, why would I ever even consider trading in the incredible woman that is my Susan, on what, by definition, must for me be a lesser model?

No, I have no desire to reclaim my youth. I'm more than happy with it staying right where it is. If I could magically snap my fingers and return to the days when my hair was dark brown and my body more like that of a Greek god than a happy Buddha, I would have to politely decline. There is so much I don't want to give up in the here and now, and so many hugs from current and future grandwidgets that I don't want to miss.

Life hasn't passed me by. This is my life! The "good old days" are happening as we speak.

About the Author

For more than 30 years Roger H. Aylworth has been a newspaper reporter and editor in north central California. His writing has earned him journalism awards for reporting, feature writing and editorial writing. He began writing a weekly humor column about 15 years ago. The columns have followed the joys and silliness of being part of a large and sometimes demented family. Roger is married to novelist Susan Aylworth (AKA "the saintly" Susan). They met during freshman orientation at Brigham Young University, married two years later, and are the parents of seven children.

We hope you have enjoyed this collection of columns. Other Delphi Books are available for the asking at your favorite bookstore, your public library, or directly from us by visiting our web site or by calling, toll-free, 1-800-431-1579.

For information about titles, please visit our website at: www.DelphiBooks.us.

To share your comments, please write:
Delphi Books
P.O. Box 6435
Lee's Summit, MO 64064
US

Printed in the United States
204914BV00002B/31-114/P

9 780976 518587